D0033051

NORTHGATE LIBRARY

OCT -- 2018

NO LONGER PROPERTY OF
SEATTLE PUBLIC LIBRARY

DRIVEN

the

never-give-up

roadmap

to massive

success

manny khoshbin

Entrepreneur
PRESS

Entrepreneur Press, Publisher
Cover Design: Andrew Welyczko
Production and Composition: Eliot House Productions

© 2018 by Entrepreneur Media, Inc.
All rights reserved.
Reproduction or translation of any part of this work beyond that permitted
by Section 107 or 108 of the 1976 United States Copyright Act without
permission of the copyright owner is unlawful. Requests for permission or
further information should be addressed Entrepreneur Media Inc. Attn: Legal
Department, 18061 Fitch, Irvine, CA 92614.

This publication is designed to provide accurate and authoritative information
in regard to the subject matter covered. It is sold with the understanding that
the publisher is not engaged in rendering legal, accounting or other professional
services. If legal advice or other expert assistance is required, the services of a
competent professional person should be sought.

Entrepreneur Press® is a registered trademark of Entrepreneur Media, Inc.

Map icon image, used under license from Shutterstock.com

Library of Congress Cataloging-in-Publication Data
Names: Khoshbin, Manny, author.
Title: Driven: the never-give-up roadmap to massive success / by Manny
  Khoshbin.
Description: Irvine, California : Entrepreneur Media, Inc., [2018]
Identifiers: LCCN 2018028449| ISBN 978-1-59918-624-5 (alk. paper) |
  ISBN 1-59918-624-1 (alk. paper)
Subjects: LCSH: Khoshbin, Manny. | Businesspeople—United States—
  Biography. | Success in business. | Entrepreneurship.
Classification: LCC HC102.5.K496 A3 2018 | DDC 650.1—dc23
LC record available at https://lccn.loc.gov/2018028449

Printed in the United States of America

22 21 20 19 18   10 9 8 7 6 5 4 3 2 1

contents

PART I

Drive!

chapter 1

this is my story

PART II

Fine Tune

▲ contents

PART III

Under the Hood

introduction

Whenever you get behind the wheel of your car, whether it's a used ten-year-old clunker or a brand new supercar, you have a set destination—a place where you want to go for a moment, for a vacation, for a fresh start in life. You can drive almost anywhere. In life, we usually have several future destinations in mind. And, just as we drive different routes to get where we need to go, typically in nicer and newer vehicles as we mature, we also follow many routes in life, some that lead to dead ends and others that lead to success.

Throughout this book you will read about the many routes I have taken and I will offer you several suggestions to keep you motivated as you travel through your own journey. Hopefully, the upcoming pages will put you "on the road" to success in both business and in life. So, metaphorically speaking, consider this book your car keys.

For those who don't know me or don't know me very well, I am Manny Khoshbin, a successful commercial real estate investor and a supercar collector who firmly believes that if you work hard, stay dedicated, and have the drive to follow your dreams, you can succeed and do great things in life.

I did not attend a fancy college, or any college for that matter, nor was I born into riches—not by a long shot—yet, here I am writing my second book. My first book, *Manny Khoshbin's Contrarian Playbook* (GeniusWork Publishing, 2011), was so titled because I am a contrarian, which means I go against the grain. The book was all about how I made a living in commercial real estate and how you could, too.

This book, however, comes in response to so many people who have seen me on social media, along with photos of my car collection, and wanted to know more about me and how I created my own path to success—perhaps in the hopes of finding inspiration for their own journey to a better life. In the first few chapters, I tell my story of coming to the United States and trying my hardest to survive and succeed. In fact, as a car lover, I see the many challenges associated with driving long distances and the long journey on the road to success. I was always working hard, trying one direction, then another, and another, and another with plenty of road blocks, detours, and disasters along the way. My journey also took me from my family's beat up old Datsun to my first car, a Honda, to a Ferrari, and on to some incredible supercars. Whether you visualize your success in buying cars, new clothes, larger homes as your family grows, season tickets to your favorite sporting events, traveling the globe, or just being able to afford nicer things for your family, you can make great strides by being motivated and convinced that better things lie ahead. So, you must keep driving forward.

I began dreaming of massive success early on in life and developed a never-give-up attitude, which is what I want you to come away with—to believe that if you continue trying, you will succeed.

In addition to my story, I also talk about staying strong both mentally and physically—staying in shape and powering up on knowledge, and never forgetting where you come from because your roots and your journey are so important. The more difficult the journey, the stronger you become. While you may not make $100 million, you can certainly reach a level of success that makes you feel good about what you do and who you are as a person. That personal, mental, and emotional strength are all factors that will keep you moving forward in that journey.

Along with motivation, I offer some advice for how to balance your life between work, family, hobbies, and the brand you build—no matter what business you are in. For example, achieving that balance calls for some practicality, especially when it comes to preserving your money—after all, what's the point of making a great deal of money if you can't have time to enjoy it? We'll also talk about some of the practical aspects of your journey such as how to brand yourself and build your team, since nobody succeeds entirely on their own.

I also talk about something near and dear to my heart—giving back to those less fortunate than you. This doesn't have to be money (it can be volunteering your time), but it is a great source of pride and kindness to help others and a way to build a lasting legacy.

I want you to get to know me, but more importantly, to feel motivated and ready to adopt a never-quit, never-give-up attitude. This book is for all the dreamers, the high achievers, and those who need a little motivation in life. Your journey won't be easy, but you need to get behind the wheel, start your engine, and **drive**.

PART I

The best way to get started on a journey is to simply start. Start your engine, rev it up, and start driving.

That's what we're going to do here in **Part I: Drive!** I'd like to start by telling you a bit about my own journey to success. As with any road trip, there have been plans, goals, distractions, and detours. But they all worked together to get me to a place where I'm not only successful in business but also content in my life. That's my hope for you, too— that you will find some of my stories from the road of life that resonate with your own experience and help you map out your own adventure.

chapter

1

this
is my
story

M journey began as many American ones do—in another country. A proud immigrant, I was born on January 14, 1971, in Tehran, the capital city of Iran. I was the second child after my sister Mahi, who was just one year old when I came along. My father was 22 and my mother 21. My father worked for a public accounting company as an auditor, while my mom took care of my sister and me. When I was two, a brother Mazi entered our lives, and we all moved to a smaller city in northern Iran called Sarab, which is where my dad served in the military. By the time I was seven, we had moved again—this time to another small city called Saveh, where my father's family resided. The city is still well-known for their pomegranate fruits. My parents bought a home, my dad opened a hardware store, and my brother, sister, and I started school. Our home was in a tract of about 30 homes surrounded by the forest. In the winter, we could see wolves coming out of the forest at night and as kids we were scared of the forest, the wolves, and the darkness.

My grandfather had a small market in Saveh where he would save the wooden boxes that the tomatoes were delivered in for me to play with when we visited on the weekends. I used to go into his backyard and build things with those boxes—it was the highlight of my weekends.

Growing up, I had two friends: Reza and Ali. We often walked to school together, which was a couple of miles from our home. Reza and I used to make slingshots and find targets to shoot at. We also enjoyed riding our bikes. We were typical kids, living out our dreams through play.

We had a happy life. It was modest and nothing fancy, but we enjoyed the peaceful serenity of living in a small town among our relatives. This was life until 1979, when everything changed. That was the year the revolution began and Khomeini, the religious leader, gained influence over the nation of Iran. He overthrew the Shah, the King of Iran, shortly after the prolonged military conflict between Iran and Iraq had begun. Open warfare started on Sept. 22, 1980, when Iraqi armed forces invaded Southern Iran along the joint border of the two nations. The war started over a conflict regarding the ownership of a river on the southern border of Iran.

I was nine at the time the war began, and I remember going up to the roof of the house with my dad and protesting. I didn't know what was really going on, but I felt good supporting my dad. I felt like a man, knowing that I could do something. Protesting was then, and still remains, a way to actively participate as a citizen.

Khomeini created the *Basij Mostazafan*, a mass movement of young people. Once in power, Khomeini issued a fatwa, an Islamic law, and a promise of paradise. The Iranian clergy took over command from the military leaders in the late 1970s through early 1980s. Then, in July, Iran launched Operation Ramadan near Basra. The clergy used "human-wave" attacks calling for young people from 14 years old and up to advance into the fields ahead of the adults to see if the minefields were clear so the army could follow. Thousands of children were killed in this horrific exercise.

This was a life-changing event for me and for all the people of Iran. My father had six brothers, but during the war, three were permanently injured and one later died from the effects of the chemical bombs Iraq used in the war. Having seen so much devastation, my father made a sudden decision to leave Iran two weeks before my 14th birthday, at which time I would likely have been forced to join the Iranian Army. He did not want to lose his son to war.

I should mention that a few months earlier my mom had given birth to a girl, Massy. I don't know how many fathers would have had the courage to make such a gutsy move, but my father wanted his family to be safe and have a better future. I still look back at this as a very heroic action on his part. We don't often realize how significant certain events are when we're young, but it's important to recognize and never forget the people (family or others) who did things that had a positive impact on our lives.

Welcome to America

It was March of 1985 when all six of us—my mom, dad, my brother (who was now 12), my sister (who was 15), and my little sister, who was only 11 months old, went to Turkey to get our visas to come to America.

Because of the urgency of this matter, my father didn't have time to liquidate anything back home, so he brought less than $2,000 with him from Iran. He had planned to start a business with a friend whom he had helped get a visa to the U.S. However, once we arrived in the United States, the plan changed as my father's so-called friend no longer wanted to do business with him, and instead decided to go work with his older brother who owned a gas station.

My father had previously visited the United States in 1984 and had bought himself a 1972 Datsun station wagon. We spent the first couple of weeks in a motel in the city of Costa Mesa, California. I remember one morning I woke up and went outside to sit by the pool. There was a little boy walking out of the pool who held up his middle finger to me as he walked past me. I didn't know what it meant at the time, so I just waved at him and patted him on the back. I did not speak a word of English. I would soon learn that gestures like that one, and many of the words being said to me by other children, were not at all welcoming.

After a while, we started running out of money, so we had no choice but to leave the motel and sleep in the car. This went on for a few months. I now sometimes drive by the Stater Brothers store where we used to park the car and realize how far life has taken us. My dad managed to get in touch with an old friend in Los Angeles. We drove up there and ended up living in their garage. We had to be quiet because if the homeowners' association found out there were people living in a garage, they would have complained and caused a lot of trouble for our friends. I remember that even though they were "friends," we were not welcome in their home and were treated with discrimination. Now, every time I meet a new immigrant from any country who has come to America and is trying to make it here, I have so much respect for them. I know how hard it is. I recognize that this nation was founded by immigrants, and if you are an immigrant in America, you need to be strong, and you may need to work even harder to achieve your goals. But you *can* achieve them.

After a couple of weeks, my father found a job with a company named Cla-Val in the city of Costa Mesa. He went for an interview and they gave him the job. At the time, the pay was only $8.00 an hour (which didn't go far in Orange County), but he had no choice because he had no work permit at the time. After a few weeks of saving money, we were ready to place a deposit on an apartment, and we moved in that August. But our financial problems were far from over. My father's paycheck would barely cover the rent and some food. So, I did what I had to do—I went to work at a very early age.

Job 1: Diving into Entrepreneurship . . . Literally

It was 1985, and my first "job," so to speak, was with my brother. We would wake up at about 4:00 A.M. and go by all the trash bins in the apartment complexes before the disposal pickup trucks would arrive.

We would pick up any junk we thought we could sell at the Orange County Swap Meet on the weekends. After a few months, we were going to other apartment complexes in the area and dumpster diving became our full-time jobs. I remember one early morning I saw a whole bunch of electronics in a trash bin. So, I grabbed the wire and pulled on it, but there was another guy in the trash bin and we started fighting over this dirty, broken radio and a toaster. Then, a few weeks later, I went to my friend's house and realized that the man was my friend's dad. I felt so embarrassed, but I think he was even more embarrassed considering he was an adult, and I was only 14.

In 1986, Mahi (my older sister) got a job at Wendy's, a fast food restaurant, to help my dad support the family. We both enrolled at Costa Mesa High School and had three hours a week of ESL (English as a Second Language) classes. Slowly, life was starting to become normal again.

Job 2: Hitting Paydirt with a Real Paycheck

In late 1986, I started working at Kmart as a stock boy for $3.25 an hour. They basically gave me all the dirty work: cleaning bathrooms, pushing shopping carts, and moving all the heavy boxes in the storage rooms. At first, I was humiliated because the other employees would make fun of my English. I even stopped walking by the cafeteria because I would hear other employees on their lunch breaks saying stuff like, "Hey, camel rider," or making other comments that I didn't understand but knew were not flattering. Some of the other employees would just laugh at me, so I avoided most of them. No matter how they made me feel, I needed the job and the money to help my family, so I showed up 15 minutes early every day and worked as hard as I could. If I was called on the PA system to help with something, I would try to run as soon as they called me, and I always stayed late if they needed me. After six months, I was promoted to assistant manager of sporting goods. I was selected as employee of the month for three months in a row and got a raise. I'll never forget, every Friday was pay day—they would pay us in cash in envelopes with our employee number written on it. And every Friday I would take $100 out of my paycheck and place it in an envelope under my bed. I was earning $3.75 an hour, saving most of it and using whatever was necessary to help my family. By February of 1988, I had saved $4,000. I went to an auto auction with a friend and bought my first car, a 1983 Honda Accord.

This was the first time that I truly realized how hard work could pay off. I dreamt of buying a car and it happened. For a teenager, dreaming of buying a car and making it happen is a success story. So, if you have kids, as much as you may want to buy things for them, let them achieve some of those things for themselves. It's also important to remember and appreciate the value of doing it yourself. Many people forget those early successes once they get rich. But I never did forget. Buying that Honda was the first of many car purchases for me, but it remains one of the most special cars I ever owned.

Job 3: Occupational Hazards

In June of 1988, I quit my Kmart job and went to work for the *Los Angeles Times* for $5 an hour. I would meet up with a group of people at a Burger King in Anaheim where we would get picked up by a company van that would drop us off in one of the local residential neighborhoods with a map of the area. Each of us would be responsible for soliciting every homeowner or renter to subscribe to the *L.A. Times* with a special promotion called "The Front Pages." This was a big book that they were giving away if you signed up for a year-long subscription. It featured the front covers of the last hundred years of the newspaper.

The job was OK except for one little occupational hazard. I was always scared of dogs, especially the big dogs, because I got bit by a German Shepherd when I was seven. So, when I came to a house that had a BEWARE OF DOG sign or was fenced in, I would look for a dog before entering their front yard or shake the fence to hear if a dog started to bark. One afternoon, as I enthusiastically approached this nice single-family residence with a fence, I shook the fence and waited for a minute as usual to see if there was a dog. Since I didn't see or hear anything, I opened the gate and approached the front door. Just as I was about to ring the doorbell, out of nowhere came this enormous German Shepherd. Startled, I dropped everything and took off for the fence as fast as I could with this monster of a hound on my heels. I managed to make a running jump onto the fence and get over it before the dog could catch me. I only got some scratches on my forearms, but that was the last day of that job.

Job 4: Life Lessons from Under the Hood

In October of 1988, my father bought us our first home in Garden Grove. My brother and I transferred to Westminster High School where I finished my senior year and got my diploma.

We had a friend named Henry who wanted to marry my sister. He was a mechanic, and he offered me a job, so I figured what the heck. Basically, we would go to people's homes and fix their cars by changing the brakes, the oil, and clutches, and then we would split the money. After about six months, I realized that he was a lousy mechanic. He had absolutely no clue what he was doing. Every time we would change an engine or transmission we would end up with five or six extra screws left over. I used to question Henry about why we had all of these extra parts lying around. He would just say, "They're not necessary. It's okay. The car will still run." I hope he is not still fixing cars. Since I didn't see much future in learning how to fix cars from someone who couldn't even set the radio stations, I decided to look for another job. There's something to be said for never being satisfied and always looking for something better until you achieve your ultimate goal, which, for me, was being a success and making a lot of money. And you know what? I still keep dreaming today! Never stop dreaming.

Job 5: Door-to-Door Sales and Sorrows

A couple of weeks after leaving the "so-called" mechanic, I got a job in WWI Industries, which was door-to-door, multi-level marketing selling dried fruits and nuts. I was one of many marketers, and they would supply us with inventory and a hand basket. We would then travel, using our own cars, and sell the goods door to door. At the time, they were supplying us with all kinds of dried nuts like pistachios, cashews, and mixed nuts in eight-ounce polyester bags. I used to go down to the local car dealers, knowing that the salesmen and mechanics loved to munch on the pistachios and that their secretaries loved the jelly beans and Jujubes. I worked for WWI for six months, and I was the top salesman at the time, but I have to say, I hated the job. So many times, the car dealership managers would kick me out of their dealerships or call me bad names. I'll never forget one afternoon, while I was selling at the Pomona Toyota dealership, the manager called me a "f---ing Iranian camel rider," then told me to get my ass out of his dealership before he called the police. This was particularly hurtful and humiliating because he did it in front of 15 to 20 salesmen and their assistants. I had tears in my eyes, and as I walked out of there I kept asking myself, "Why do I have to set myself so low just to make money in this country?" Why was I subjecting myself to abuse just because I looked different and came from another country—especially considering that this country was built by immigrants? But I picked up my basket and as I walked out I told myself, "It's OK. I will show them. I will grow up and be rich one day!"

Job 6: My First Business

As it turns out, walking away was the best thing I could do at the time. One day, while I was shopping with my parents at Price Club (now Costco), I realized that bags of nuts were selling at almost a fourth of the price that WWI was charging me.

I thought, "If they can do it, why can't I?" Why couldn't I disrupt the business model of multi-level marketing and venture out on my own—for a much lower cost. I did the math and realized doing so was entirely possible. Since the profit margin was so high, I started my own business, Unlimited Wholesale Products. This was right after graduating high school, so I had plenty of time to create a job for myself. I leased an 800-square-foot office space, with two small partitions, on Knott Avenue in the city of Stanton. I would buy all the goods from Price Club and repackage them in eight-ounce polyester bags, seal them with a heat sealer, print labels from my dad's computer, label the bags, and I was ready to go. I would then place a lot of flyers near the payphones in search of a sales force. After about three months

I had four people working for me, and I was making $3,000 to $4,000 a month. Not bad for an 18-year-old!

Essentially, I was doing the same thing as WWI. I would sell the bags to my salesmen, and they would sell them door-to-door. One day at lunch, I walked into a restaurant with my basket of nuts and sat down to eat a hamburger. As I was taking my first bite, a gentleman, probably in his 40s, came to my table and asked what I was selling, so I explained the different type of nuts and candies I had. He bought three bags for ten bucks, and I was so happy to make a sale at lunch. What I didn't know was this would be the end of my new-founded business. The next morning, he was in my office asking for my health permit. Turns out, he was a health inspector having lunch after inspecting the restaurant. It was my shitty luck, I guess, but it did teach me a good lesson about making sure your business is compliant with local laws and ordinances. It was an important step that I overlooked at the time and learned not to in the future.

I didn't have a health permit; I didn't even know it existed, so he fined me. The requirements to bring the space up to code were costly, so that meant I was out of a job again. It was, however, my first attempt at being an entrepreneur and it started me off with a very simple premise—rather than creating something from scratch, which is often more difficult to do (not to mention time consuming), find something that you can buy at a low price and sell for a higher one. Over the years, I built upon that simple "buy low and sell high" premise by adding value in between the purchase and the sale. This is a basic concept when it comes to selling that you should always keep in mind.

Selling nuts door-to-door taught me a lot about people but even more about myself. It helped me grow and tore down a lot of my fears and barriers.

Job 7: Moving Up and Moving On

Having no great ideas for another business, I found myself looking for a job once again. This time, however, I decided to call the manager of a Winston Tires store to whom I used to sell nuts. He was one of the few people I'd met who wasn't racist, and he even asked me to come in and meet with him to talk about possibly working for him. While I was at the meeting, he called the company's headquarters and put in a good word for me. I got hired as an assistant manager at Winston Tires in 1990. I was only 19 at the time and was earning $1,700 per month. It didn't make me rich, but it was good, solid money at the time.

I worked at the store in Buena Park for three months and became one of their top salesmen. Then, out of 180 assistant managers in the company, they picked me to run the Montebello store, where sales were below their projections. They believed in me and wanted me to help boost their sales. Finally, I was getting some hard-earned respect.

While I was slowly building up my career, I also fell in love. It just so happened that it was with my sister's best friend. Her name was Sheila. Unfortunately, she moved with her family to Michigan. Then, a couple years later, they moved back out west, to San Francisco, and stupidly, I drove up there with my parents to propose to her. My parents went along because where we come from, it is a tradition for parents to approve of the marriage. Not only did she turn me down, but her mother told my parents that I was not worthy of their daughter—that I was young, uneducated (no college) and, specifically, not rich enough. Apparently, my success wasn't good enough. I was crushed and heartbroken. Once I got over my broken heart, I had added motivation to show her and her mother that I could become a success. So, once again, I got up and pushed forward. Rather than responding to doubters and negative people by losing faith in myself, I used such negativity as added motivation.

Jobs and More Jobs

Luckily, I was always able to find a new job. I was resourceful and determined to find something that I liked and something that would pay off for me. Over the next three years, I continued to find new opportunities. During the year I worked for Winston Tires, I managed to save about $10,000. That money would prove to come in handy for my next venture.

At this point I started doing research, something that will always benefit you before making your next business decision, and learned that the Mobil Corporation was planning to upgrade their pumps and tanks in the near future. So, my father and I entered into escrow to buy a Mobil station, knowing that once they did the upgrades, the value of the station would at least double. We found an agent who guaranteed that I could buy the station worth $160,000 with just $10,000 cash (in hindsight, I should have been skeptical). So, I signed the purchase contract and went to Rancho Cucamonga to become a Mobil dealer. After paying $3,500 in fees to Mobil and three weeks of training, I passed all tests and got my dealership license, which I still have in my office today.

The problem was that my financing never got funded, the loan officer turned out to be a crook, and the seller didn't want to sign the extension for escrow, so I lost my initial investment. I had been played. At that point, I had nothing left. I was driving a Dodge Omni that I bought for $500 with a passenger door that didn't even open. (As you probably realize, cars have always been a passion of mine, so I vividly remember what I was driving at various points in my life. I had moved up to a nicer car, but still had much fancier cars in mind.)

With no job or any business ideas, a friend suggested I go to an insurance seminar. After two months, I got my insurance license and started selling life and health insurance. It was a bad idea that didn't suit me, so after three months I called it quits. Who wants to be talking about death benefits every day?

I wanted something more positive. And more profitable.

Enter Real Estate

I had a friend named Ben who owned a successful mortgage company, so I took a real estate course, got my real estate license, and took a job working at his company. I liked real estate and thought it was something in which I could grow and make good money. So, after four months I opened my own company with another real estate broker named Matt. We moved to a large office with panoramic views. I was only 21 when we first started our mortgage company, Century West Financial, and things took off quickly. I must admit, I was stoked to dress up in fine suits and drive a Mercedes, which I bought after the first three months of business. That was my first luxury car. It was also the beginning of new chapter in my life, or so I thought.

The following year, 1993, was probably the best year in every way for me. We made a lot of money (over $290,000 in loan fees and commissions), and I bought myself anything that I wanted. I had a Mercedes, wore lots of fancy suits, and was finally comfortable financially.

Then, in 1994, Alan Greenspan raised interest rates and everything turned around. Our refinancing business was slowly sinking, and it wasn't very long before we were forced to shut down the office. But by then I had spent most of my money on my car, fancy suits, and dining out. I learned that when you're killing it at your job or in business, you need to diversify your earnings and save for a rainy day. In hindsight, I should have taken some of my earnings and started investing in real estate. That's why I advise you to invest first and spend later. Don't forget that nothing good lasts forever.

At this point, Matt and I decided that we should invest what was left of our money so we would have something to fall back on in case the market really dried up, which it did. In April of 1994, we each invested $50,000 in a new discount store concept where everything was the same price. These stores have gained wide popularity since, and we were in the mix from the very beginning.

We opened a 79 Cents Plus store in Santa Ana, which did very well. By then, I bought a '92 Lexus LS400 and finally moved from my family's home in Garden Grove to a nice town house in Irvine. I bought myself all the goodies from electronics to fine crystal to an 80-gallon fish tank. I even custom ordered a blackjack table. I remember one day I walked into Circuit City, a huge electronics retailer, and spent $11,000 on a big screen TV along with all kinds of speakers. My partner Matt got married to his longtime girlfriend, whom he had been dating for five years, and they bought a house in Irvine. Finally, everything seemed perfect.

The Day That Changed My Life

On March 24, 1995, I got dressed up as usual and went to a restaurant and club where I was supposed to meet some friends. After waiting for a while, they didn't show up, so I went to the Empire Ballroom where there was a Persian party going on. While I was there, I noticed a woman whom I had once been interested in dating, though it never panned out. She was dancing all night with another guy (not that she wasn't supposed to). However, it was troubling to see her, so I started drinking with two good friends that I had run into at the club, Gary and his brother Steve. At around 1 A.M., Gary asked me if I could take his brother Steve home and, being a nice guy, I told him that I would. Gary wanted to stay at the club a little longer because he had just met a woman there. So, at about 1:30 A.M., I settled my tab at the bar and went to get my car from the valet. At that time, I noticed Steve was with a friend of his, John, who also needed a ride home. My car was a two-seater and it didn't dawn on me that there were three of us, so I agreed to take them both home. I told the friend to hop in, and he could sit on Steve's lap. So, we took off from Empire's parking lot and headed south on the 405 Freeway. I had had the car for only two months at the time and being young and stupid, I decided to show off. I was speeding with the top down when I saw the exit that we were getting off at. I tried making a quick turn to exit the freeway, but I was going too fast. Having had a few drinks didn't help matters any, and I lost control of the vehicle. Both passengers were thrown from my car.

It is with great pain that I tell you my friend Steve died that night from a severe concussion to his head. John survived with only some minor scratches. It was truly miraculous that I wasn't injured at all. That's the part of this story that makes me feel so guilty and still upsets me. I came away without a scratch. That made it so much more difficult, and I harbor a great deal of survivor's guilt to this day.

▲ chapter 1 / this is my story

Sometimes I wish I had been hurt, because it seemed so unfair that I lost a friend because of my carelessness.

My life changed 180 degrees after that night, and I cannot express how much pain still drills through my mind and body every time I think of my good friends and their families.

After the accident, I went into a deep depression and went to see a therapist since I was having a very hard time dealing with what had happened. I also went to Alcoholics Anonymous for a while, not because I was an alcoholic, but because it was my drinking on that night that made me responsible for what happened.

In October of 1995, I was sentenced to the Nancy Clark rehabilitation program, which is an alternative sentencing program. It was kind of like a halfway house. I was there for nine months and on five years' probation. I have to say I was very lucky. Life has its moments of happiness and sorrow, and sometimes you can't undo your mistakes and the pain you cause for other people.

For me, the pain that Steve's family will carry for life will always be in my heart, and I have asked God to please forgive me and to reduce the pain for his family. I tell people to be grateful for what you have because nothing is forever. I have visited his grave with flowers several times, and I once took a blackjack chip and placed it on his grave. You see, I was at his one-hour photo shop earlier on the day he died, and I was telling him about the blackjack table I had purchased. I invited him to come over some time to play and he replied that he loved blackjack. We never got the chance to play cards together, so I took a chip to his grave because I thought then (and still do) that he was a winner.

The recovery program helped me a lot; it has made life a lot easier for me. I can now open up to my friends and family and talk about my problems. I later purchased my first home in Garden Grove for a good cause: an alcoholic recovery home. I called it "The Last Resort." I had it for a year and was forced to sell it due to mismanagement and because I could not afford the negative cash flow any longer. Though it did not succeed, I'm grateful for the opportunity to try to make a difference. It was the first time I made philanthropy a part of my life, and it helped me recognize the importance of giving back—especially when you've gotten a second chance at life.

Spiraling Downhill

By December of 1995, Matt and I had lost about $40,000 in our second 79 Cent Plus store in which we had invested $120,000. I started borrowing on credit cards just to get by. I sold my Mercedes and moved into a one-bedroom apartment in Irvine. Needless to say, 1995 was a very dark year for me, and the following year didn't prove to be much better.

In 1996, we closed our second store and decided to convert our first store in Santa Ana to a Mexican supermarket. We spent $100,000 to reopen the store. Just our luck, a big chain called Food 4 Less opened a store right next to us. Our sales kept on going down and by 1997 our store started losing money. Matt and I finally put the store up for sale. By 1998, I owed $180,000 on my credit cards and was paying $2,500 a month in interest alone. Matt was coming to work less and less, since we weren't making any money.

Meanwhile, I was working seven days a week, 15 hours a day just to keep the business from failing. I finally told Matt that either he needed to buy me out, or I would buy him out. He said he didn't want the store, so I settled with him in 1998 and had to assume all the outstanding liabilities of the store. I knew I had to do something. At that point, I had a negative net worth and the store was the only thing I had.

Somehow, through all of the difficult times, I managed to maintain an attitude that somehow it would all get better. I had no choice but to work hard for myself and for my family. Taking ownership of the store was a risk, but as my father had taken a risk in getting his family safely out of Iran, I knew I, too, would have to take risks in life, and I've ended up taking a lot of them.

YOUR ROADMAP TO SUCCESS

► First, it's important never to forget where you come from. It's important because it keeps you humble.

► You need to have resiliency and a never-give up-attitude. I was determined to pursue my dreams and kept looking for some way to become a success.

► Save for a rainy day. Invest first, spend later.

► Don't throw your success around or flaunt it.

► Learn from your mistakes. I learned a lot from losing my friend; it was a horrible lesson, but it's one I cannot forget.

► Alcohol or drugs are not the answer.

2

success
at last

Unlike many other personal success stories you might read, you'll notice I did not spend my years at the finest schools. I did not go to Wharton or Harvard, nor was money set aside for me to go to any college, much less graduate school. Instead, I attended the school of hard work and experienced many disappointments along the way. For me, it was a long journey. Remember, I started working at the age of 14, saving up whatever I could and helping support my family. I had no time to take a break along the way. Work *was* my school.

You see, in life, you really have to figure it all out for yourself, which means you need to learn whatever you can any way you can (remember, this was before the internet). For me, learning the math and the details of buying and selling helped out a lot.

At some point during the late 1990s, my parents had moved to Oregon because my father had gotten a job offer. But, at about the same time that I bought out Matt, my dad lost his job there.

Realizing the value of having family working together, I asked them to move back to California, and they did. At this time, I had 13 employees in the supermarket, so I let eight of them go and had my mom and dad work with me. My mom was handling the register and my dad took care of the paperwork. It took several months before we started to have positive cash flow. Then I started to advertise a lot and got the sales up by 40 percent. When the business was finally doing well I sold the store for $285,000. After paying my vendors, I was left with $185,000. Finally, after several very difficult years, I was able to resume the career I had begun years ago: real estate.

My First Commercial Building

I was finally able to return to real estate and reopened my mortgage company only this time I started with a small overhead. I paid off some of my credit cards and with about $130,000, I began buying stocks on E*TRADE, such as AOL among others. I more than doubled my money in ten months. I felt like this was too good to be true. So in September of 1999, I pulled most of my money out of the stock market and bought my first commercial shopping center in Whittier, California, which is not too far from East L.A. It was a shopping center that I bought with $200,000 cash down. Then, a few months later, I bought a house in Santa Ana for my parents to move into. At the time they had been living with me in my rental in Irvine so it felt good to be able to give them their own space.

Meanwhile, my mortgage company was doing well and I finally had enough savings to start a new venture: buying fixer-upper homes to remodel and sell. Not unlike that first venture selling nuts and dried fruit, I was buying something at a low cost and reselling it for much more. This was a simple model that proved to be lucrative for me. Remember—buy low, increase the value, and sell high for a profit. It works for real estate as well as it does for nuts.

As it had in years past, my personal and professional lives worked in tandem. A few months later, I met a beautiful Persian girl named Nadia at a Turkish restaurant and club. She had just come out of a bad relationship and did not want to date, so we became good friends.

At the time I truly felt like there was more to us, so I got an apartment in close proximity to where she worked so that I could invite her over for lunch. For about eight months to a year, I hardly did any work—my world revolved around her. In time, as I had hoped, our friendship turned into a relationship. And on February 2, 2000, I asked her for a commitment, and she accepted. I was so in love with her, and I knew I wanted to marry her.

Then, on January 26, 2001, I got down on one knee and proposed to her. She said yes, and in September of 2002 we got married. Giving our relationship a strong foundation was important to me, and the experience taught me that a successful marriage must be built on friendship, trust, and loyalty.

My First Million

In September of 2000, I was at the post office in Santa Ana, just two blocks from my old store, looking at this great shopping center across the street that had been abandoned for two years. Deep down I knew the center was a goldmine, and I always wondered who owned it, and if, one day, I could buy it, remodel it, and open a new discount store. As I left the post office that day, I noticed a man trying to open one of the doors of the old shopping center. It seemed odd since it had been vacant for so long. So, I drove across the street and asked the man if he was the new owner of this center and he said, "I work for a bank, and just hours ago, we foreclosed on this property." My heart was about to jump out of my chest. I knew I was looking at one of the greatest opportunities of my life. I quickly got out of my car, shook his hand and introduced myself. Then I asked if he had any more information on the property. He replied that he didn't know what they were going to list it for, but he gave me the name of the real estate agent who would handle the sale of the center.

I immediately called the agent, but he knew nothing about the shopping center. He told me he would have to call me back. Apparently, I beat him to it. I called him again that same day and asked him out to lunch. We met the following day. I told him that I was a real estate agent and if he could work out a sweet deal for me then he could have my commission, which would have been an extra $20,000 for him. He told me that the bank was in it for the $850,000 loss, and they wanted to get this off their books by the end of the third quarter. I knew right away that I had to make an all-cash offer quickly to get it at a low price. I told him to write an offer for $500,000, and he laughed and said it was too low.

I told him to write it with no loan contingencies and 30 days closing. He was impressed, and so he did. The bank countered with $750,000, so I told him to give a final and last offer at $675,000, which the bank accepted.

I knew the bank was not in the business of real estate sales. They're in business to lend money, and this property was not only tying up their money but was, in fact, actually losing money for them. The bank took my offer, and I wrote a $10,000 check from my Wells Fargo line of credit for the deposit. Would you believe I did not even have the $10,000 in my account at the time? I had to borrow from my line of credit to open escrow. Once we opened escrow, I went to "loan sharks," (hard money lenders) to get all of the money. My plan was to put up my Whittier Shopping Center in which I had at least $300,000 equity and borrow the rest from a retail bank. This was getting complicated— but I knew the reward would be worth the risk.

Two weeks went by and I started getting nervous. I had less than 15 days to come up with $665,000. My money was all tied up in two homes and the shopping center. I had $40,000 to $50,000 in stocks and that was it. My mortgage company and realty sales were not doing very well, so I went and saw an old friend who recommended I get 90-percent financing through the Small Business Association (SBA) and referred me to an approved lender whom I'll never forget. He was about 75 years old and knew SBA loans like no one else. After giving him the short version of my life story, he fell in love with me and told me that he was going to help me out. So, he approved my SBA portion of the loan at 40 percent of the purchase price. I still needed a bank to lend the first half of the purchase price and that would leave it to me to come in with only a 10 percent down payment. He then referred me to a banker, J.P. Swift with El Dorado Bank, for the rest of the loan.

Working with Manny
J.P. Swift, Banker

The first time I financed a deal for Manny was when he needed a startup loan for an ethnic food market. He bought the building and had big plans, but the city made it very difficult for him. He had to retrofit the property and make sure it met their standards. The process took 18 months. It was tough on Manny and tough for me to carry that loan during the time it took to renovate the property up to the standards the city required. Nothing seemed to be good enough for them, which made it take much longer and cost more money than we had initially expected. Ultimately, when he was done, he was offered a price for the building that made it more economically feasible to sell and make a profit on it. The funds from that property were used by Manny to kick start the building of his empire, or his portfolio of properties.

We worked together on other deals after that first one. After he started buying, fixing up, and selling properties in Arizona and in Texas, the downturn in the economy enabled him to get back into the California area where he now has his office in a building that I financed for him.

What stands out about Manny is that from 10,000 feet you could say he got lucky and benefitted from rising real estate values, but when you get to know him you can see that he has a keen understanding of the market, and he knows what he's looking for. When he buys a property, it's a property in which the value can be increased through working smart. He does not rely on what the market does, so if he had a million in the bank or $50 million in the bank, his work ethic and his approach would not change.

I see that hard work and the dedication and commitment that it takes to achieve what he's been able to achieve. Manny learned what worked and didn't work. This made the next move he'd make that much better. He never stops learning and working very hard. Plus, he's very smart.

So, I met with J.P. and told him my story and that this property was meant to be mine. I had been eyeing it for years and it was a perfect fit for me, so after a two-hour meeting, he gave me his approval. This was my second victory, and I knew it was almost a done deal. The only problem was that the SBA takes 60 to 90 days to give their approval before funding the loan. OUCH. What was I going to do?

One of the requirements of the SBA is having an occupancy permit, which I went to the city to obtain. While I was there getting the permit, I found out that the building had a substandard lien on it from the city. What happened was that the previous owner took out a load-bearing wall, which rendered the building unsafe. Also, since it had been vacant for over two years, the city required the property to be brought up to code for everything, including landscaping, earthquake retrofitting, handicap access, and parking. This building was not going anywhere as it was. I immediately went to the agent, told him the story, and explained to him that I was ready to close but the property was not sellable due to some substandard conditions and the bank had to bring this building up to code or it would be in breach of our contract. The bank replied that they would go down to the city and take care of it, not knowing this would not be a simple task. After their efforts failed, they tried to cancel the escrow. That's when I hired an attorney and forced them to sell the building to me or I would sue for liquidated damages. The bank was being bought by a larger bank at the time, and I knew they did not want bad publicity. So, after weeks of litigation, they agreed to do the modifications to the structure and get the lien removed so that we could get the occupancy permit.

The repairs for the structure cost the bank over $100,000 and took a year. During this year, rates had gone down, and the refinancing business was doing great, so I made a bundle of money in my mortgage company and saved over $150,000. I had the money and my SBA loan was ready to go. The bank tried to cancel on me since they knew the property was now worth at least a million dollars and the city was forcing them to put in new landscaping and earthquake retrofitting. Once again, I called my attorney, and we forced them to continue the escrow. I even got them to credit me $67,000 for additional upgrades required by the city. Then, in March of 2002, after 18 months, I closed my escrow. I immediately got two bids on all the remodeling jobs and started work. I spent $200,000 on the property and sold it in June of 2002 for over $1.6 million. This was my first real big break. I had one million dollars in cash and for the first time in my life I felt like a millionaire. Wait a minute—I *was* a millionaire!

Looking back at the entire experience, I can tell you this: if you reach that definable breakthrough moment in your career or in life, don't let any obstacles get in your way. Do whatever you need to do to make it happen. There were several times I could have thrown my hands up in the air and given up. But I knew this shopping center was a potential goldmine, so I kept working to make it happen. I fought for it. Not every deal will come through—but you'll never know until you've done everything you can to make it happen.

A Hot Market for Commercial Real Estate

With $1 million cash at my disposal, I started buying apartment buildings in Long Beach, California, in cash and a very short escrow, so I was getting all the good deals. I bought a nine-unit building for $550,000 and, after remodeling it, sold it for $895,000 four months later. In one year, I had turned $1 million into $2 million.

By 2003, the California market was starting to get tight, so I began to look in other states that presented better value. I found a property in Phoenix, Arizona, one weekend when my wife and I were in Palm Springs on vacation. I remember suggesting to my wife that she should go to the spa and do some shopping and that I would go tour the property and be back by early evening, so she took off for the spa and I drove from Palm Springs to Phoenix for a tour of a building that I was interested in possibly purchasing. I liked what I saw, negotiated a deal, and drove back the same day. It was a total of eight hours of driving, but I was so excited about getting the deal that I wasn't even tired. I made an all-cash offer with limited escrow and little-to-no contingencies. I guess you could say my wife and I both did some shopping that day.

In Phoenix, I only bought depressed office buildings with at least a 70 percent occupancy ratio. My first office building acquisition was in June of 2003, the one I drove from Palm Springs to tour. It was a 36,000-square-foot building, and they were asking $1.5 million. I got them down to $1.325 million and ten days in escrow. A few months later, in December of 2003, I bought a four-story medical building in Phoenix for $4.66 million, but this time I got a loan on it since it was a great building and had great cash flow.

To make a long story short, a lot of California investors started to buy in Arizona and the market got hot. By the end of 2004, I had bought and sold over $30 million worth of real estate in Arizona and had turned my $1 million into $17 million. All in all, this was pretty good for a guy who spent several weeks living with his family in a car and started a career rummaging through trash bins looking for anything to sell for profit.

For me, this was a freedom that I had never felt before. That year, I bought my parents a four-acre ranch (my dad's dream) in Fallbrook, California, which is in San Diego County. I wanted to thank them for all they had done for me, bringing me to the United States and doing everything they could to take care of me and my siblings.

I also threw a private party for my wife's 30th birthday and bought her a big fancy yellow diamond ring and, for Christmas, a brand new Range Rover. I bought myself a Ferrari Spider, a brand new Rolls-Royce Phantom, and a Ferrari F40 supercar. I was a long way from that old Datsun. By now, I learned my lesson from my prior years when I spent most of what I made on cars and shopping. This time, I promised myself that:

1. I would only splurge on luxuries when I had invested enough to have excess cash flow beyond my living expenses.
2. I would buy using only the excess cash flow from my investments and not from selling any assets (my nest egg).

As you can already tell, I love cars, and this was the first time I was able to really treat myself to everything I wanted. For me, the cars and the expensive ring for my wife's 30th birthday were symbols of achievement. It was not to show off—it was to celebrate. I believe if you work hard and it pays off, you should be able to treat the people around you, and yourself, to some of the things they've always wanted. I also believe in helping people and believe in the saying, "what goes around comes around." After all, we are all here as guests and can't take the money to our graves. I know a lot of wealthy people who have become slaves to their wealth. My philosophy is work hard, play hard, and live the life of your dreams. But never forget to make investing a priority. I always told my family, "If you daydream your dreams, you're halfway there. The other half is making a plan and working at it." Of course, you can get there much quicker with a little bit of luck.

Doubling Down

I started buying a portfolio of properties from REITs (Real Estate Investment Trusts) and private investors who wanted to get out or trade up or down. I then sold them separately for a profit. In November of 2004, I flew to Houston and made my first purchase on a portfolio. It was a three-building portfolio I bought for $10 million. Then, four months later I sold it for close to $14 million. That was my biggest gain on a single transaction at that time. What was funny was that I bought it from one private fund and sold it to another private fund. You are probably asking how I did it.

There are various factors, but the most important part of buying and selling real estate as an investment is the timing of the markets, which I was able to identify after researching the areas for the deals I made in Phoenix one year prior to investing in Houston. Then, it's finding a property that you can add value to. In this case, these properties had very high operating costs and high salaries for on-site building engineers and managers. I fired them and was able to hire more reasonably salaried staff, and I also bid out the utilities for much lower rates. You need to do a lot of research and look for trends in any industry. Once you become good at spotting markets on the upswing or downswing, you will become better at predicting what may happen in the near future. However, you always need to keep in mind that this is NOT an exact science. But, learning your industry and watching it very closely day in and day out can give you an edge when it comes to buying and selling. Then, you need the fortitude, and guts, to pull the trigger on a deal. Of course, it's important that you have "extra" money beyond what you need to support your family.

Knowing an industry and being able to read it to act quickly when you see a deal or an opportunity is one thing, but having a passion for that industry is something else. I wanted to do something I really loved—after all, you spend so much time working, you should love what you do. This was something I kept trying to figure out.

Quite honestly, for the first eight to ten years, I was still a bit confused as to what I should do for the rest of my life. I now know that real estate will be my life. No matter what else I get involved in, I find myself coming back to real estate, my passion, where I've been very fortunate and have enjoyed great success. An old Jewish friend once told me that if you take some soil, put it in your pocket and come back in 60 years it will still be there and God is not making any more of it. It means that the world isn't growing (expanding) but the population is, so the property that you have will still be there and it will be in greater demand (and more valuable) years later.

That always stayed with me, because it not only speaks to real estate, but motivation as well. For me, the "soil" I always carry is my lived experience. For example, a journalist who once wrote an article about me pointed out that those months of living in our car stuck with me and built my desire to succeed in real estate. That memory remains with me, and I tap into it throughout my journey.

My First Real Estate Investment Fund

By May 2005, I had close to one million square feet of office buildings valued at over $70 million under management. I was flying high and everyone that knew me wanted a piece of the action, so I opened The Khoshbin Fund I, LP. This was an investment fund for which I raised $3 million and bought a six-story building in Amarillo, Texas, for $9.5 million. It was known as the B of A building because Bank of America was the largest tenant.

I don't even fly to places like Amarillo when I buy properties. Today, I can go online to places like www.LoopNet.com, a multiple listing service for commercial properties, where I can search for buildings based on certain criteria.

> "We all have the capability to be whomever and whatever we want in this life. It is just a matter of having determination, persistence, patience, and the will to follow through."

Around the same time, I also formed The Khoshbin Company, which is my management entity and was also the general partner to the funds. By now, I was very excited and was looking forward to my future.

I went from struggling and being ridiculed, disrespected, and treated as if I did not belong, to someone who has doctors, lawyers, and CEOs of major companies coming to see me about making investments. I learned that working hard and becoming successful at whatever you do makes people respect you more. It's not just because you have money. People in wealthy families are handed money. It's because you've worked hard to get where you are and because you never gave up on your dreams. That's what makes me feel good about myself and can make you feel good about yourself, too.

YOUR ROADMAP TO SUCCESS

▶ Don't let obstacles get in your way—find (legal) ways around them.

▶ If you find a major breakthrough—something that can change your life—go for it, fight for it, and don't give up!

▶ Remember, in sales it's always about buying low and selling high, no matter what you're selling.

▶ Study the markets in which you plan to invest very carefully, and only invest money you can afford to lose.

▶ Look for markets that are depressed and properties that are poorly managed when you choose to buy, and be patient—sell later on, at a time when people have money to spend. While you sometimes need to act fast, having patience is very important when investing, especially in real estate.

3

detours along the journey: from devastated to elated

The year 2005 started out to be a great year. I had close to two million square feet of commercial real estate under management, and the market was starting to heat up. I was excited about the possibilities. With the formation of The Khoshbin Company, I was able to take control and manage my portfolio in-house. I was busier than ever working more and more hours seven days a week. Unfortunately, I didn't realize how this was affecting my marriage and it fell apart. I was totally caught off guard. I wasn't around much, so she was bored and lonely, going out and partying without me. In the end, I paid a heavy price for spending so much of my time chasing success and money.

To put it mildly, I was devastated. I never thought I would be one of those guys that had been divorced, but there I was. My parents had been together for so many years and endured so much, yet they stayed together. I guess I just thought marriage was forever. In this case, it wasn't, and I had to accept it. We had known each other for five years and had been married for three. Thankfully, we didn't have kids so no one else had to suffer through this. Having kids would have made the divorce more painful.

I then realized I would have to start all over again. For the next 12 to 18 months, I buried myself in my work, exercised constantly, and went out at nights with my single friends. I have to admit, a lot of times I tried to numb my pain at bars with friends and at nightclubs. Divorce was one of the most difficult battles of my life to overcome besides living in a car in extreme poverty and losing my good friend in the car accident. However, as time went on, I realized that my wife and I had nothing in common. We were really not all that compatible. I still felt bad about the breakup, but knew I wanted someone with whom I could share common interests and have a family with.

By mid-2006, my divorce was final, and I had met a woman named Juliet who soon became my girlfriend. She was a dance teacher and was very kind and sweet. However, our personalities did not align, and we often clashed (perhaps I was just tainted from my failed marriage). We met through a mutual friend and enjoyed great companionship during my difficult post-divorce years, yet I guess I kind of knew this was not going to end in marriage. In time, we decided to go our separate ways. During that time period, I had moved out of my home and rented a penthouse condo at $6,500 a month. All of my friends kept asking me why I was renting since I owned so many commercial properties. I told them the market cycle was at near peak and that a big recession was coming.

The Writing on the Wall

In 2006, business was still very good and my climb up the real estate ladder continued as I kept buying up value-add properties (commercial fixer uppers), fixing them up, and leasing them out to tenants. By late 2006, I started to see the writing on the wall—there was a huge downturn ahead. I had been following the markets closely for a while now and had become pretty good at seeing signs that the markets were going to turn around. I was able to get a sense of what was likely to happen next. And, since the economy goes in cycles, it looked like the strong economy was coming to an end.

Each time I would list a property for sale, there were more and more out-of-state buyers with 1031 exchange money bidding up the property. When you sell a property in the United States, you can choose to do a specific kind of exchange, like a 1031, and defer the taxes on your capital gains by buying a like property. Since property values had been going up in California for several years, investors in the state were selling and had to buy new property to defer their gains, so they started looking in other states, like Arizona or Texas. I had been buying in Arizona a few years earlier and had sold my properties by 2005. I then started buying in Houston. At the time, the price of a barrel of oil was very low, and since it was an oil town, Houston was struggling economically so there were some good deals on property.

As more and more people were trying to jump into the market, I could see it was starting to overheat with higher prices and too many deals. It could not last. I remember my first visit to Houston in early 2004. I flew out to tour three buildings that a private fund, Caldwell Watson Real Estate Group, was selling. I found these properties online, and they seemed to be great value-add candidates, low price per square foot, a little underperforming on occupancy, and carrying high operating expenses as they were managed by a fund. I saw this as a great opportunity since I could add value by bringing the occupancy up, lowering the operating expenses, and thereby increasing the net income—and as a result, also increasing the value on resale. I arrived at the airport and the listing agent picked me up. He asked, "Is it just you?" I said yes. Apparently, a lot of buyers show up with their team, but I was quite comfortable handling deals on my own—not that I didn't get outside advice from my own team members when reviewing potential deals, but I would often go on the property tours by myself.

We headed to see the buildings during a three-hour tour. Afterwards, he showed me a five-building portfolio listed. The next day, the listing agent dropped me off at the airport, and I flew home.

A day later, I emailed him my offer of $9,650,000 for the three midrise office buildings, they accepted, and we opened escrow. Then, after doing my due diligence, we closed with me putting just 25 percent cash down. Now that the deal was completed, I went to work. First, I flew back to Houston and let go of the onsite property managers who carried high salaries, and I bid out all the vendors for janitorial, AC, parking, and security. By doing this, I was able to reduce the operating costs by 20 percent. Next, I started an aggressive leasing promotion and got a few new tenants. Long story short, I raised the value of the properties and went on to sell the same three buildings six months later for approximately $14 million. Honestly, I had no idea I would sell them that fast as I intended to keep them longer. But when I saw the huge increase in the net income and how the buildings had stabilized, I decided to move on to another value-add property. Once the properties sold and were in the news, Fred Caldwell called me. He was anxious to know how a young man from California came thousands of miles over to Houston, bought three properties that they had owned for five years, and flipped them in six months for a profit of over $4 million. So, he asked if we could do lunch. I was flattered and accepted, so we met for lunch the next time I was in town, and we had a great conversation about real estate investing. It's always important to take the time to build relationships, no matter what industry you are in, but especially in real estate. Remember, business is all about people.

In 2005 and 2006, I went back to Houston to hunt down other properties to which I could add value. I had built a great relationship with my banks and in the Houston market. In the next few years, I went from owning three buildings to nearly 60 buildings, totaling two million square feet of rentable space. I did this by looking through hundreds of listings for the best value-add properties. In some ways, it was easy for me to identify a property that carried higher operating costs and lower occupancies than other buildings in Houston. In some cases, I did major improvements, as was the case with a 12-story building I purchased in East Houston. I didn't like the exterior color, so I had it painted black and put mirrors on common areas of each of the 12 floors. The look of the building was changed for the better, and I was able to attract a higher quality of tenants. Again, you need to buy low, add value, and sell high—it works in any kind of sales. Following that approach helped my bottom line. And, since oil is a big part of Houston's economy, rising oil prices helped create a larger pool of qualified buyers.

By early 2007, I decided to list all my properties in Houston and sell them. I knew there was a short-term demand uptick and an opportunity to sell at the highest price. People were buying in a market that had gotten way overpriced, which was the case with many markets throughout the country. Prices can only go so high before everything comes crashing down. Unlike the many buyers trying to jump into the rising market, being a contrarian, I knew this meant it was time to sell and get out of the rising market. By mid-2007, I had sold over $100 million of properties in Houston. I found a very active broker, Darrell Betts, with whom I decided to list my portfolio. Darrell and I had a great time together and enjoyed a successful working relationship.

The Great Financial Storm Makes Landfall: The "Great Recession"

By selling most of my risky assets, I was able to raise cash and move my investments into safer assets, such as long-term leased, grocery-anchored shopping centers, and institutional quality industrial parks, which typically weather the storm much better during recessions since these come with tenants who have stronger credit and are more vested in their space. That's what saved me during the recession. Most of the office buildings I sold ended up in foreclosure. In business, it's important to be forward thinking and be ready to act. I saw a major adjustment coming in the real estate market, so I acted before the recession hit.

Then, sure enough, in October of 2008, shit hit the fan, and the recession came roaring in. We all know how bad things got. It went from a seller's market to a buyer's market relatively quickly.

No one knows for sure when economic cycles will turn around, but when you see the writing on the wall as I did, it's a telltale sign to start preparing for the worst. Fortunately for me, I had sold my Houston properties and had money to spend. The next few years from 2008 to 2011 presented one of the greatest real estate buying opportunities in history. I actually got a little too excited and bought too early. In just three months, I purchased 25 single family homes all in distress sales or REOs (real estate owned, which is another way of saying bank owned). One of these properties was a house that I purchased and moved into with my second wife, which you will read about in the coming pages. The home had been appraised for $9.2 million prior to the recession. I purchased it for $6 million. As you recall, the market continued to go down with a wave of financial institutions also breaking down and sinking with it. They would later need government bailouts or find themselves filing for bankruptcy. Meanwhile, I continued to buy. Looking back now, I remember wondering when we would get back to the peaks. I had seen several recessions in my 20-plus years in real estate, but this one seemed far worse than the others; it felt like the nation's second great depression. The way I saw it was simply that if this was the end of the world then everyone would lose everything; but if we all survived, then I would make a fortune.

As it turned out, I went on to buy back most of the buildings that I had sold in 2007 in Houston. I bought them back from mortgage companies for a fraction of what I sold them for. Being a buyer, these were the price reductions of a lifetime. For example, there were two buildings I had sold for a total of $34.5 million in 2007 that I bought back in 2012 for $17 million. I then sold them again in 2015 for $24 million. Had it not been for the oil crash of late 2014, I would have probably gotten $34 million again, but you should never get greedy when you are doing very well and I say you never go broke taking a profit. Remember that. Too many people think that when things are going well, the upswing will never end, but guess what? It will. So, get out, take a profit, and keep moving forward. My destination, my goal, was to become very successful. I had accomplished that—life was very good, but I kept on dreaming—in my business life and in my personal life.

The Love of My Life

A lot of people say that God has a plan for you, and maybe they are right. Even though my first wife broke my heart and I was in pain for over a year after our divorce, I never would have met the true love of my life if we hadn't gone our separate ways.

In 2007, as the recession neared, and I was busy selling off my properties in Houston, I met a Persian woman named Leyla Milani at an event in Newport Beach, California. She was there making a celebrity appearance. She was already well known from her years as an actress and, more notably, as briefcase model #13 on the NBC hit game show *Deal or No Deal* and having also been in some movies and television shows, such as *Rules of Engagement*, *Las Vegas*, and *The Tonight Show with Jay Leno*.

I had come to the event with a few friends of mine who kept saying to me, "Don't you know her? She's the only Persian model on this huge game show. You've seen her, right?" They made a big deal about her, but I didn't know of her at all. As we hung around the event, my friends all went to take photos with her and got me to join them and take a photo. At the time, I was still dating Juliet, so I wasn't interested in asking her out, but I had to admit to my friends that I was immediately blown away by her beauty and her charisma.

Fast forward two years, after Juliet and I had broken up, I looked up the name Leyla Milani on Facebook, and, sure enough, I found her. I wrote to her, saying it was nice to meet her online and asking if she remembered the photo we took together several years back, knowing it was a long shot since it had been two years. She did not remember it, so I sent her the photo my friends had taken of me standing with her at the event. We went back and forth online for a couple of weeks messaging each other. She had seen photos of my car collection and I was amazed by how much she knew about cars. To my surprise, she was a big car aficionado, and we discussed

Our Shared History

Leyla Khoshbin, Entrepreneur and Spouse

Manny and I share a lot. We share a beautiful family, a love for entrepreneurship, and a lovely life together. But one thing we also share and care about deeply is the story of how our journeys dovetail. We have both experienced life as immigrants, which has informed how we approach business and life.

Like Manny, I moved from Iran at an early age. My mom left my abusive father and moved my sister and me out of Iran to Toronto, Canada, when I was nine years old and my sister was only six months. We knew it was hard to come to the United States, so we settled in Canada first and my mom worked there as a registered nurse while raising us as a single mom. She thought we'd have the chance for a better life and a better future in Canada and then, later, in the United States than we would have ever had in Iran.

Since my mom was out working, I took care of my sister a lot. I took on the responsibility of being the disciplinarian and the tougher one as we grew up. I became that father figure in our home since we didn't have our dad. In many ways, it turned out to be a good thing for me because I grew up really fast, but in a good way. Manny and I share that. He knew early on that he had to make his own way in the world, as did I. And that responsibility was a good thing for us both. Having such a responsibility kept me out of trouble—not that I was prone to getting into trouble, but I didn't have the time or desire to go out drinking with my friends or do reckless things like some of my peers. I became focused on finishing school and working to have a better future, just as Manny was laser-focused on making the world of business his school.

We both had strong role models in our parents. I saw how hard my mom worked, and I respected her for that. She showed me how to be the boss of my own life. I also always knew that I wanted to have a great quality of life, so I surrounded myself with people like me who were also ambitious. That's where Manny and I have a lot of similarities. We are both very disciplined, strong-minded, and we make our own decisions. Nobody really tells us what to do; we are our own motivators, you could say.

Eventually, my family moved to Los Angeles because my mom always dreamed of living there. She was drawn to the glamour of Hollywood from what we saw on TV. In time, her

Our Shared History, continued

dream became my dream, too, and I attended fashion school and went on to create my own clothing line, then moved on to acting.

After working as a model in music videos and on shows like *Entourage*, I landed a gig on *Deal or No Deal*, which proved to be a fortuitous event in our shared history. It was after the show ended that I met Manny. I got to know him and realized very quickly how different he was from most of the other men in Hollywood. You think when you look at the photos of him with all of his cars that he has the "Hollywood" lifestyle and is a big shot, but he's so much the opposite. He's a true family man with a heart of gold. He does post a lot pictures about his cars, but it's not to boast—it's truly his passion and something he loves. He has a lot of passion for work and life, and it's amazing and inspiring. What attracted me to him was that we connected at a higher level and shared so much in common from cars and family to our entrepreneurial spirit and a strong, determined belief in ourselves. It also didn't hurt that he was living in Orange Country, which is more family-oriented, and not as crazy as Los Angeles.

And just think—two immigrants from Iran both chased their dreams to California and ended up together. And that's what we are—together in life, together in business, and together as parents. I see how he is with our children. They adore him, and when he comes home, they jump all over him. He loves being around them.

So, as you read Manny's story, I hope you'll take away all of his great advice. While commercial real estate is his forte, the lessons he shares here apply to anyone who is starting or scaling a business. But, more importantly, I hope you'll take away something from his story, which is ultimately a story about the power of tenacity. It is an immigrant story. It is a uniquely American story. It is OUR story.

Lamborghinis and Ferraris at length. She complimented my Ferrari 360 Spider, but said the custom yellow wheels had to go. At the time she had a new Mercedes sport coupe, a CL500, which she had customized. I remember thinking, "Wow! This girl really knows her stuff." I thought it was unusual for a beautiful woman like

▲ chapter 3 / detours along the journey

her to have such an interest in, and knowledge of, cars. Plus, she was incredibly self-sufficient and successful in her own right. She mentioned that she was coming down to my area for her friend's birthday and that if I wanted to, I could stop by the party so we could meet in person. I did, and we ended up talking for two hours that night. Our connection was undeniable. The chemistry was spot on, and I guess it's true when they say, "When you know, you know!" That was just the beginning. We dated for a few months, and I proposed to her six months later on my birthday in 2010. You could say I "closed escrow fast!" She was completely surprised and ultimately gave me the best birthday present ever by saying, "YES!" We were married on July 22, 2011.

One of the things that brought us closer as a couple was working together. Yes, I know that can often be a bad thing for a relationship, but it has worked well for us. Leyla was always known on *Deal or No Deal* for her lavish big hair, referred to as her "lioness-like mane." People thought and to this day still think she wears hair extensions, but she doesn't and didn't—her hair is 100 percent natural. I must admit that even I didn't believe her at first until I ran my fingers through it. That remarkable hair helped Leyla decide that she wanted to launch her own hair care business capitalizing on her trademark hair and fame from the show. So, she researched the best real human hair extensions on the market and outsourced a company in Asia to create the best quality hair extensions with special clips so it would be less visible when you wore it. She had other ideas as well, and essentially reinvented the hair extensions market. When she started sharing her business plans and ideas with me, she told me that she was meeting with a famous hairstylist in Los Angeles about going into business together. She said he was going to put up the money for 50 percent of the ownership. At the time we were still dating, but I told her I'd go into the business 50–50 with her. She agreed, and we became partners in business before we became partners in marriage. Her business, Leyla Milani Hair, opened early in 2011, and I knew it would succeed; she's very smart and creative and takes the lead from developing the product to sourcing and designing the packaging. She's also a great business partner. She knows far more about the beauty industry than I do, but I know about finances and try to advise her in that area. Sure, we've had some business disagreements, but for the most part, we get along quite well in business as well as in marriage. Combining her vast knowledge of the beauty industry and dedication with my business experience helped us work smart and grow the haircare line. And, in just a few years, Leyla Milani Hair became a multi-million dollar business.

In 2012, we went from being partners in business and partners in life to also being partners in parenthood when our daughter Priscilla was born. If our life together wasn't busy enough, we knew it would now get a lot busier. And then in 2016, our son Enzo was born. Yes, Enzo as in Enzo Ferrari. I wanted to name him Bugatti (ha, ha) but just couldn't convince Leyla. I was truly elated to have become a father not only once but twice!

I have to say, having kids gave me a whole new respect for parents. It's a full-time job, especially if you want to be good, responsible parents. I no longer work on weekends and rarely past five o'clock during the week, as I learned that in order to maintain a marriage, and be there for your family, you have to have a balanced life. You need to split your time between your family and your work. We'll talk more about how to balance your business life and your personal life later in the book.

My life has changed a lot over the past twelve years. I went from the pain of a divorce to a great marriage and a wonderful family. Business also took off as I was able to time the market well and buy and sell as a contrarian prior to, and during, the recession.

YOUR ROADMAP TO SUCCESS

▶ Keep your eyes and ears open to what's going on in the market and pay attention to the winds of change and patterns that may be emerging.

▶ Don't stay idle when you see opportunities. Yes, there are bumps along the way, but you'll never reach your destination (business or personal), if you don't start driving and keep driving forward in life.

▶ Sometimes you need to swerve quickly on the road—you may also need to swerve away from potential danger in the market. If you see bad signs ahead, get out while you can. If I had not gotten out of Houston and sold most of my properties, I would have crashed and burned like so many investors.

▶ Remember, things can, and will, change dramatically throughout life. I went from being devastated after my divorce to being elated by my second marriage and the birth of my children a few years later.

▶ Remember, if you don't stay driven and continue on your journey, you won't have the full life experience.

PART II

Finding great success in my business and personal life put me on top of the world. As much as I wanted to be wealthy and find someone with whom I was meant to spend my life, nobody could have promised me that my dreams would come true. No matter how hard you try, there are no guarantees.

Once you have success, you want to maintain it. I've seen many people reach goals and dreams only to see them disappear. Today, I continue to do the things that helped get me to where I am today. I know that if I stop, things could go south quickly.

It's all about constant self-improvement and self-maintenance.

It's like having finally attained the car of your dreams, a beautiful car that you love to drive. But what happens if you do not maintain that car once you own it? It will not look as stunning as it does when you first bought it, and it certainly will not run as well. You need to keep your engine fine tuned and continue to do car maintenance, just as you should keep your mind and body fine tuned and do the necessary maintenance to your mind and body.

In the next few chapters, I discuss several aspects of life that are so important for reaching your goals and maintaining them, from surrounding yourself with positive, inspiring people, to taking care of your body and mind with exercise, to expanding your mind by absorbing knowledge, to dreaming big about your future. Remember, like owning a fabulous car, you want to make fabulous dreams come true and keep on living that dream.

what
keeps
me going

As you can see from Part One, mine was a difficult journey, filled with ups and downs and detours along the way to becoming successful, but I was determined to make it. I always chose to look forward rather than dwell on mishaps or misfortunes. Life, like driving, is best experienced with your eyes on the horizon—not looking in the rearview mirror. My never-give-up attitude is all about the mindset. Train your mind to be positive, curious, and resilient. In other words, look for the good in any situation, explore life's possibilities, and develop a "bounce back" mentality.

Today, people see how successful I am, and they often make one of two assumptions: some people think that I must have gotten very lucky while others assume that someone dropped a real estate business in my lap. While everyone who is successful has some element of good luck in their life, I have also had a lot of bad luck along the way, going back to having my mixed nuts business shut down by the health department and later getting defrauded by a loan company on the purchase of a Mobil gas station. I started to see success with my supermarket only to have a large supermarket chain open up next to me and almost force me into bankruptcy.

> "Failure is not an option—it's part of the journey."

I had one disaster after another and went from business to business before enjoying real success. When you read other people's success stories, this is often the case; it took a while until they found their road to riches. For me, that road came through real estate.

Once I started making money, it did not get easier. Nearly every deal was rife with challenges and difficulties. I had to fight to close deal after deal. In fact, recently I purchased a $29 million waterfront commercial property that was anchored by a high-end restaurant that had spent over $5 million on improvements. The community was so excited for the restaurant opening but within a year they had to close down, and after months of searching for a credit operator to take it over, the deal collapsed. It took me nearly a year, and another $2 million, to finally find a new tenant for that space. The point is, while I have been very fortunate, it has not been an easy journey.

For me, hard work and the belief that it would all pay off has always been my mantra. I knew there were great opportunities in America, but I also knew as an immigrant kid I would have to work even harder to achieve my dreams. I had no other choice. But I also really wanted (and was excited about the opportunity) to continue getting out there day after day to keep chasing my dreams.

Chasing success in each business endeavor became my passion. I was never someone who waited around hoping success would just fall into my lap. That doesn't happen. Very few people win the lottery, but many people are successful through hard work. I knew that when I started out, and I still believe it today. And if you still want to play the lottery, you should note that nearly 70 percent of lottery winners lose it all and file for bankruptcy. So, you're better off putting in the hard work.

If you are just starting out on your journey, there are certain things you will need to make the trip. I liken them to having sufficient fuel, oil, good tires, and a well-honed engine to get started en route to your destination. Along with hard work and a belief that you will finish your journey, there are three basic elements that you need from the start of your trip—basics that you should never lose sight of along the way.

Element 1: Remember Where You Come From

One of the reasons I told my story in the first few chapters is because I never lose sight of it. It's part of who I am today. When people ask me, "What kept you going through the major ups and downs that you've endured over the years?" I tell them that I never forget where I came from. Living in a car and digging through garbage bins makes you try hard and develop the right attitude, which is not simply, "Just be positive, and everything will work out." Instead, it's, "Despite the inevitable setbacks, I will never, ever give up. I don't ever want to go back to that!" Looking back through the years, as I became more and more successful, that mantra helped me stay motivated.

When you have that mentality, you won't get any surprises. You have to think like a warrior or like a fighter and keep on battling. Then, when something goes smoothly, it will be a bonus. It takes time to really develop this mentality, and I must admit that the more you struggle in life, the tougher it is to maintain a positive attitude. But you also gain strength from those experiences. If you give up, you will never know how much you can accomplish. Remember the saying, "That which does not kill us makes us stronger."

Sometimes, you need inspiration to develop that toughness, whether it's from sports heroes, military heroes, or the heroes we watch on television or in the movies. I remember having come to this country as a teenager; I used to watch the *Rocky* and *Rambo* movies. I really connected to the character Rambo trying to fight his way out of a hole. They were movies of victory, of fighting for what you believe in. I also connected with Arnold Schwarzenegger, who had also come to this country as I had, although under much better circumstances. They both had a never-say-never, never-give-up attitude no matter what. Even when I ran my supermarket in the late 90s, and the large supermarket-chain opened next to my store and my sales got chopped in half, I did not give up. I had to sell my car and my home to feed the negative cash flow of my store. Everyone around me told me to file for bankruptcy and start all over with a new venture, but that was not an option for me. I knew this country was built on hard work and credit . . . and at that point, hard work, credit, and my reputation was all I had. For me to file for bankruptcy was like death!

Most people grow up with challenges to overcome, whether it's poverty, difficulties at home, single-parent families, emotional challenges, physical challenges, being bullied, having few friends, drug or alcohol abuse, physical abuse, facing bigotry or prejudice (which I can relate to), or several of the above. While some people want to forget their roots and their past, others want to remember so they can gain strength from where they've been and what they've been through. By contrasting where you've been with where you are, you can see how far you have come—even if you've only taken baby steps on your journey.

Stay Humble

Your background also helps keep you grounded and humble. You don't want to dwell on the challenges that you've been through, nor do you want to feel sorry for yourself. It's very easy to make excuses. "I wasn't born into a wealthy family, so how can I succeed?" or "Look at my childhood. How can I ever believe in myself?" Yet, there are countless success stories of people who have pulled themselves up from no place to reach, and go beyond, their dreams. Consider that Jennifer Lopez was homeless and slept on the couch in a dance studio and Oprah Winfrey was raised by a single teenage mom in poverty. James Earl Jones overcame a stuttering problem to become one of the most well-spoken actors in Hollywood—even doing the voice of Darth Vader. Richard Gere was a struggling actor for 20 years before making it big in movies like *American Gigolo* and *Pretty Woman.* Jerry Yang lost his dad when he was two, and later moved with his mom and siblings to the United States from Taiwan at age eight, knowing only one word of English (shoe). He went on to become the founder of Yahoo! A young

Steve Jobs used to return Coke bottles for money and had his meals for free at the Hare Krishna temple. J.K. Rowling endured poverty, losing her mom, and single parenthood (she even lived in her car, as I did) before creating the Harry Potter books.

The point is, you need to be fueled by where you have come from. It gives you greater motivation to work hard. Even if you came from a wealthy background, you more than likely had your own personal struggles in life.

Remembering where you came from also benefits you in another way—it makes you look more closely at the people around you. To this day, I can feel the pain that many young immigrants have to deal with, especially at this point in our country's history. I know because I heard the names people called me and remember how I was treated when I was younger and how it made me feel. We all come from somewhere, and that informs how we navigate the world. Remembering my journey from Iran and my early life as an immigrant helps keep me grounded and reminds me to pay my success forward by showing kindness in both business and my personal life.

Element 2: Exercise—Building That Fighter's Mentality

Along with the never-say-die attitude I got from movies like *Rocky* and *Rambo* was another one of the fundamentals of my life, exercise. It is one of the key factors to my success. I remember when I was a teenager and bought some dumbbells for a dollar each and started working out regularly. I knew I wasn't going to become a bodybuilder, but it gave me a connection to Rocky, Rambo, and the movie characters who refused to back down. They had to fight to survive and to get out of the situation they were in whether it was boxing or combat. In my own way, it gave me a sense that I, too, could be stronger, physically and mentally, and fight my way out of a hole.

Over the years, I found exercise to be critical in my life because every time I lost self-esteem or hope, I always went back to the weights. Now, three decades later, I still maintain a regular workout regimen. Today, I work with a trainer three times a week—rain or shine. I do so whether a deal has gone well or has come crashing down. You don't

have to have a trainer; you can set up a
simple routine of three sets of pushups,
sit-ups, and go for a jog. For years, I did
sit-ups and pushups when I got out of bed
each morning.

*"It doesn't matter what type
of routine you choose—just
make a commitment and
stick to it."*

Most people think of exercise as fitness
for the body, which it is, but it's also
fitness for the mind. There are so many other benefits of exercising
regularly. You've probably heard or read numerous times that exercise
can reduce stress and relieve anxiety. But it can also motivate you to
be active, productive, stay focused, and even creative. The body and
mind work together. I've found that exercise makes me feel better
mentally and emotionally. You are able to forget your problems and
immerse yourself in your fitness routine. While many people turn to
alcohol when things get difficult (and I must admit that I have done
that on occasion), I have found that exercise has always been a far more
productive alternative for getting me through some bad times in life.

Exercise was there for me back in 1998 when I officially reached
a negative net worth, owing $180,000 on my credit cards and had
no assets other than my supermarket, which wasn't worth anything.
I remember when I was trying to sell my supermarket, which wasn't
going to be easy (my sales dropped by 50 percent), and my family
kept telling me that I was not going to win against a supermarket
chain with 40 stores. They reminded me constantly that I could not
get into a price war or I would lose everything. In fact, my own family
and friends were telling me that I should file for bankruptcy, but I
would not do it.

So, after moving into that small one-bedroom apartment, I kept
working seven days a week from 6 A.M. to 9 P.M. By the time I counted
the money, closed the registers, and put the money in the drop boxes,
it was 9:30 at night, and I was exhausted. Then, after my 15-and a-half-
hour work day, I would drive twenty minutes to a 24 Hour Fitness
and run on the treadmill every day, and I would just keep saying, "I'm
going to sell it, I'm going to sell it, I'm going to sell it." And then,
finally, after an exhausting year, I sold it and actually did well. I felt

kind of like a boxer in the ring who refuses to go down. I saw myself as Rocky Balboa. I didn't want to throw in the towel. Exercise day after day was the key to keeping me going. It was my motivational tool. I may have done a few hundred miles on that treadmill, but it all worked out in the end.

Fitness Can Be Therapeutic

Fitness was also there for me when I went through my painful divorce. I set my focus on working hard to overcome the personal pain of the divorce. I was working seven days a week and at all hours. Being single again, I went back to hanging out with my single friends—but I really had to go back to the drawing board to get myself motivated. It's just the way things go in life; sometimes you get knocked down and you have to get up and start over again. To do so, you need to focus on what motivates you. For me, lifting weights and exercising was a big part of it. It had helped me before, and I knew exercise would help me again. So, I also returned to focusing on my workouts at the gym when I wasn't working. Some people will turn strictly to alcohol or drugs, and rather than motivating themselves, they try to bury their feelings. The problem, however, is that if you spend too much time drinking or on drugs, you're only masking one problem and starting another. At least by throwing myself into my work and into my fitness routine, I was trying to forget the pain while doing something beneficial for myself. For about six months, I tried to focus on my work and my workouts. Sure, I was still hurting, but after exercising I would feel rejuvenated mentally and physically and would start working again. No, exercise won't make painful experiences go away, but it can help you refocus on what's important in your own life and help you stay focused on the present rather than dwelling on the past.

Conversely, exercise was also there for me during the best times of my life: meeting my second wife, getting married again, and starting a family. It gave me time to focus on what I had and helped me appreciate life. In good times, I continue to exercise to maintain a sense of well-being. It's an "addicting" activity that can be very good for you.

I recommend that you start slowly with your exercise routine, as I did with my dumbbells, then build a routine slowly. Come up with a routine you like, whether it's with weights, a stationary bike, running on a treadmill or on a track, or any combination that works for you. The key is to promise yourself you will stick with it no matter what. I found a gym that was inexpensive and was open during hours that would accommodate my schedule. I would go there to work out on days I was tired, busy, happy, or sad. No matter what, don't let yourself make excuses for not exercising. It takes willpower to keep going three or four times a week, but after the first few months, it gets easier and easier as it becomes part of your life and you begin to feel the results. You'll feel good about yourself, not just from the actual exercising but because you have committed to self-improvement. Yes, exercising can teach you discipline and build self-confidence as well.

Element 3: Surround Yourself With Positive, Successful (or Like-Minded) People

If you want to be a good boxer, go up against the local champion. You may lose, but you'll learn a lot. If you want to succeed in business, you'll also need to learn from people who've done what you are trying to do.

I always chose older friends who were more successful than I was. I was always one of the poorest guys in the group, but I knew I could learn from them. Also surround yourself with like-minded and positive people. Like-minded means you have similar goals—not necessarily the same, but you are both striving for huge success. As for being positive, that is very important. Positive people believe they can accomplish things and are ready to go the distance. Negative people find excuses, while positive people find solutions. You'll hear this from many motivational speakers—they tell you how important it is to be around positive people. But it's not about just saying positive things or for "rah rah speeches," it's because positive people have good ideas. When other people say, "I give up, let's just go get a beer," the positive person says "We can make this work. Let's try a, b, and c." Even in a bad situation, positive people find something good as a takeaway.

Networking Matters

When it comes to surrounding yourself with successful, like-minded people, networking is also very important. I started well before networking became a buzzword. I was always meeting new people who would then introduce me to their friends. For example, back in 1991, I was out with some friends when I met Ben, I asked him what he did for a living and he said he owned a mortgage company. So, we talked a little about what that entailed. When he left, I saw him drive off in a Porsche. Being a car enthusiast myself, this was someone I was not going to easily forget. Over the following year, Ben and I became friends. He was a smart guy, and I wanted to know his secret to success. After all, he was pretty young to be driving a Porsche, and I was driving a ... well, it doesn't really matter. We had similar interests, and he was a positive person.

In time, we became friends. Then, when a con artist took me for a lot of money when I was trying to buy my gas station (remember that story from Part 1?), I called him and told him what happened, hoping he could help me get my money back. Instead, he told me that he'd love to hire me. He said I seemed like a really hard working, motivated guy. So, I went to his office, he started me off in his company, and that was how I learned all about loans. As I mentioned earlier in my story, I liked what I was doing so much that about four months later, I opened my own mortgage company. And it all happened because of networking.

I don't suggest surrounding yourself with successful people in order to take advantage of them, but simply to learn from them. Some people will be more than happy to help you, and teach you, while others will see you as a threat or simply not have time for you. Don't get frustrated. Instead, keep on looking for good people who are where you would like to be and get to know them. These days, it's very easy to reach out to people given all the social media platforms available for networking.

Speaking of that, I have many contacts on social media and numerous followers, which is wonderful. Your inner circle, however, are the core people whom you know and trust. They are people who believe in you and see the positives. They are success-minded, not just in business, but in life. You do need, however, to convert your online contacts to real relationships, and be very, very selective in the process. I made my contacts in the industry from real-world experiences before the era of social media. And those are the connections that have stuck for the long term.

One of the people who encouraged me to go into real estate was my landlord at the supermarket. As was the case, other than sending checks to his company, we got to know each other while sitting in a courthouse after being sued by a potential buyer of my store who had put down a $15,000 deposit and had 30 days to do his due diligence, which had expired. That didn't stop him from trying to sue me to get his $15,000 back. At the time, I was in my twenties and my landlord was around seventy, so I didn't really expect us to become good friends. As we started talking, I remember him saying to me, "You're a young fellow. Why are you working seven days a week and basically slaving away? Why don't you start investing in real estate?" He knew I was struggling since I was occasionally late with the rent, so perhaps he didn't mean I should jump right in at that time. He told me how he got into real estate and added that I reminded him of himself when he was younger.

My landlord said he had come to Southern California during the 1950s when it was mostly orange groves and strawberry farms. He purchased a little shack in Santa Ana for a small amount of money—then he bought another one, and another. Forty years later, he ended up owning 30 or 40 buildings in Santa Ana. He assured me that in the long run, real estate was the way to go. I thanked him for the encouragement and told him that when I was ready, I would call him.

It was about a year later and several hundred miles on the stationary bike before I finally sold the supermarket and made $185,000. At the time, the stock market was doing very well, and I had a lot of friends seeing tremendous returns. This was the late 1990s and the dotcoms and tech stocks were going wild, so I opened an E*TRADE account in 1999, bought a bunch of stocks like everyone else, and watched as my account more than doubled in ten months.

Knowing how volatile the stock market could be and knowing that it couldn't go crazy forever, I took the money out, picked up the phone, called my old landlord, and told him that I was ready to get into real estate. He sent a broker to see me who had worked for him for many years and was a good friend of his. The broker brought information about three very good real estate options for me to look at, and I bought one of them. The landlord was the same person who told me that if you put soil in your pocket and come back 60 years later it will still be there. That's what you have with real estate—something that lasts—and I never forgot his words.

Another successful person I became friends with was Tom, who had a positive influence on me and impacted my career. I also met him

My Saving Grace
Carla Reid, Property Manager

I met Manny shortly after he had purchased a property at which I was working part time. I had retired from Ford Motor Company a number of years earlier and had taken on a part-time job on this property.

When Manny came in to see meet me, he said, "Carla, I bet you have enough knowledge of the property, being here four years now, that you could be my property manager."

I told Manny, "No, I don't want to do that. I've seen the property manager do that job, and it's not easy." But Manny was convinced for some reason that I was the right person for the job. So, at the age of 69, I became his onsite manager for a very busy, lucrative property that he owns in Newport Beach. That was in December 2015, and I've been doing the job ever since and really enjoying it.

As I watched Manny over the years, everything I've seen out of him is just amazing. The way he handles himself, how he deals with people, how he works with his employees, and so on. He's like no one I've ever known in my life. He has been my saving grace, pushing me

chapter 4 / what keeps me going

My Saving Grace, continued

onward and upward and encouraging me to do more. After I thought my career had died down, I suddenly had a whole new career in property management.

Most recently in November of 2017, I had to go out on medical leave because of serious problems with my eyesight. Although I had been to some excellent physicians, he told me, "Carla, we need to get you a second opinion. Don't worry—I will take you on a plane to get a second and even a third opinion if necessary. I will also foot the bill." I didn't know what to say except thank you.

So, one morning, Manny picked me up at my home and took me to John Wayne Airport where we boarded a plane to Salt Lake City. Manny had been referred to Dr. Randy Olsen, who was recognized around the world for his research on eye problems at John Moran Eye Institute.

Once we were there, Manny didn't leave my side. He escorted me to see the doctor and stayed with me all day as I went through studies and evaluations by doctors there at the university. I can't imagine being so blessed in my life to have Manny there to help me.

For him to put his time, his money, and his efforts into bettering my life was truly amazing. These things just don't happen to most people. How can I not be thankful for him? Manny is such a humble and kind person, and Leyla, his wife, is just an angel. So, I give them a standing ovation.

As for me, my eyesight is now recovering. Dr. Olsen told me it would be a year for that eye to heal after so much trauma (I had previous surgeries), and the eyesight that I have regained has been miraculous. He hopes I will be regaining more of the sight in that eye as the year progresses.

So, after being out of work a few months, I returned to my job as property manager, doing shorter days and taking public transportation because I was not quite able to drive yet. But I'm getting there, and Manny is so proud to have me back on site. I am so blessed to have met someone like him — such people are so hard to find.

during the days running my supermarket. Tom was someone from whom I ordered much of my merchandise. He knew I was a hard-working businessman, but he also knew the supermarket business was not easy, so he gave me 30-day terms for all invoices. I remember one day when a woman doing his accounts receivables called the store and a guy working for me answered the phone and told her that the store was under new ownership, and I was no longer there. Tom panicked and called me, thinking I had sold the store and run off with the money without paying my balance. Little did he know, I had called his office and gotten the balance owed and deposited the total amount in his company account. Needless to say, he was very surprised.

Tom, as it turned out, owned a bunch of real estate in Vernon, California, including his own warehouse, which was kind of like a Costco. He told me he was buying another building in downtown L.A. and the seller wanted $2.5 million, but that he made an offer of $2 million and told the seller that he'd pay in cash. The seller accepted the offer and they closed in roughly ten days with no contingencies. I learned the importance of making deals quickly from hanging around with Tom. In fact, I like to go one step further than he did. If I really like the property, know I can add a lot of value, and that there's a lot of "meat on the bone," I will often just go in and write a $200,000 non-refundable deposit check to the seller, subject to a clear title of course. I've used this strategy to do six or seven deals quickly on properties I really liked because I thought they were gems. It's a way of letting the seller know that you are convinced you want to do the deal. Essentially, you make it really hard for them to say no.

By surrounding myself with good people who were experienced in business and real estate, and knew more than I did, I was able to learn about the business while getting the encouragement I needed. Had I surrounded myself with people who were terrified of real estate and had only horror stories to tell me, I might never have gone into the field that I grew to love. I always liked real estate, but these individuals who believed in me and showed me how they had made it, played significant roles in my success. No matter what you are trying to do, surrounding yourself with likeminded and successful people can benefit you immensely. The encouragement you'll get from people who have been successful is very motivating, no matter what industry you are in.

 YOUR ROADMAP TO SUCCESS

▶ Train your mind to focus on the positives. Also stay curious, and be resilient, ready to bounce back and try again. I know, this takes time and some practice.

▶ Remember where you come from to stay humble.

▶ Look for inspiration: I found it in movie heroes. Wherever you find it, hold onto it and use it as fuel for your journey.

▶ Exercise regularly—it helps you escape the negatives and enjoy the positives of life while invigorating both the body and the mind.

▶ Surround yourself with positive and successful people. By getting to know people who are successful in what you want to do, you can learn a lot. I did. It also gives you the motivation to follow in their footsteps.

5

dream
big

If you're going to dream, and we all do, why not dream big? After all, if your dreams are very ordinary, your life will be very ordinary. So, dream for a bigger and better life. Picture yourself in the home of your dreams, driving the car of your dreams, visiting other parts of the world, working at something you enjoy, having great success, or enjoying time with your family. Whatever it is you want in your life, dream big and set goals to make those dreams come true. Elon Musk dreams of going to Mars, and he's working on it. Personally, I think it's more beneficial to keep your dreams earth bound, but to each their own.

The trick is to find something you are good at and keep doing it until you are living your dream. I know, that's easier said than done, but as you can see from the early chapters about my life, I kept trying and trying to discover something I liked doing and could be good at. Finally, I found real estate. You, too, will find your niche.

Once you discover what it is you excel at and can clearly see your dreams, plan to reach your dream. Think of it like setting your destination for a trip. You need to figure out the route to get there, and unfortunately there is no GPS for reaching your dream destination. Therefore, you'll have to ask yourself and research whatever that may be. For example, what does it take to become the conductor of an orchestra? A successful architect? A restaurant owner? A United States senator? A movie producer? The CEO of a Fortune 500 Company? A real estate mogul? Do the legwork and learn everything you can about your dream goal. Then, get ready to get going.

Setting Goals

After you establish what your dreams are, it's time to set your goals. Ask yourself what activities can get you to living your dream. And just like you don't want to have ordinary dreams, don't set average goals for yourself.

> "Average goal-setting techniques create average results."

Be aggressive with your goals. Consider where you see yourself in one, two, five, or even ten years. Then, set your sights on realistic goals that you can 100 percent accomplish each year. These goals should be moving you closer to your dream. They should also be very clear and written down so you can look at them. Remember, you can't drive from point A to B in the dark. So, turn on the headlights by planning every step of the journey to achieving those goals.

When I came to this country my dream was to be a success and make a lot of money to help my parents who struggled for so long. I also wanted financial freedom for myself, which meant having enough money so that I did not have to depend on anyone else. True financial freedom means having control over all of your finances. Over the years, my dream came true, and I gained financial independence. I also had enough money to buy my parents a ranch so that they could retire. Another dream of mine was to own a nice car. That meant so much to me. At one time, I recall living next door to someone who owned an exotic car dealership, and I always saw new Ferraris parked outside. Owning one of those Ferraris became

▲ part II / fine tune

one of my dreams, but I told myself I would buy it when I had enough cash flow from my properties to buy it in cash. The dream became a reality after years of investing when I finally had enough to spend $325,000 on a red Ferrari F40, my first "supercar."

There's No Magic Formula

The problem with big dreams is that too many people think they will somehow magically appear. They really don't want to work for it. They'd prefer to find the pot of gold at the end of the rainbow, or win the lottery, which has only slightly better odds than finding that magical pot of gold that does not exist. Truth is, the lottery isn't a dream that you can work hard to achieve—it's something that could just happen by luck—it's a fantasy. Since you have no control over it, you can't do anything more than buy a ticket and hope for the best. Gamblers may dream about winning the jackpot, but for the vast majority, it remains a dream and nothing more. The dreams I'm talking about are those that are attainable; they may require a lot of hard work and trying various ways to get there, but they are realistic and achievable over time.

Remember, dreams are like destinations—if you want to go somewhere in life you have to recognize where you are and visualize where you want to be. That's the key to success: to stay motivated, you have to keep dreaming. If you don't have any motivation, you won't have a destination. My thoughts and my imaginations today are my distant reality. They are the dreams that I believe I can achieve.

It's More Than Money

Dreams are not only what money can buy you. Money is a marvelous tool that enables some of your dreams to come true, but there's more to life than just acquiring money. For example, I dream about helping other people and I'm fortunate to be able to give to charities and help others, including family and friends. Helping people is something I truly enjoy.

People have all sorts of dreams—some are about what they want to accomplish in life. Some people dream of climbing Mount Everest, others dream of being an Olympic athlete, or perhaps running in the Boston or New York Marathons. Even athletes dream of doing something they haven't done before. Olympic gold medalist Apolo Ohno dreamt of doing the grueling IRONMAN competition, which is the ultimate test of physical strength and endurance all in one long event. It was quite different than being a speed skater. He achieved the dream a few years ago—it wasn't easy, and he did not win, but he completed one of the most grueling physical challenges for any athlete. Why? Because it was a dream of his.

For me, I now set challenges for myself. For instance, I started dreaming that maybe I could be one of those people who creates something new in technology. It was not about the money anymore. It was about the challenge of doing it and making a product that actually filled a void in the market. That was what led to Fuzul, an app I created that would essentially allow me to utilize other people's cell phone cameras anywhere in the world (we'll talk about that more later). Even in real estate, I dream about what I can do with a property. It's kind of like an artist looking at a blank canvas or a lump of clay. I look at a building, and I see what I can do to it to make it more desirable, to increase the rents, and then to sell it. It's a project and a challenge, and I love it.

I also have a dream of someday mentoring five to ten high school or college kids at a time in business, kids who are really hungry and want to be entrepreneurs. I've received a lot of letters from people who want me to mentor them or who want to shadow me. It would be great to help the next generation of entrepreneurs. But, with two young children and a tireless schedule, this is a dream I can only start when I'm older and my kids are grown.

Find Your Sense of Purpose

Dreams give you something to strive for. They give you a sense of purpose, and if you don't have a purpose in life, you'll likely get depressed and sit around sulking. Just like you need to stay hydrated to do physical activities, you need to stay motivated. Dreaming big keeps you active and moving forward in life. Very often, people make money and get too comfortable—they have a family, a nice house, a fancy car, they go on vacations, but they also get depressed. They don't have a destination anymore; they don't have dreams. So, I tell people to never stop dreaming. The former athlete may dream of becoming a coach, a manager, or a business owner. The burned-out attorney might decide to become a law school professor and shape the next generation of attorneys.

My advice is to make a vision board of your dream life, and always be thinking about what you'd like to do next once you achieve each dream—what is your next big dream? For example, many retirees don't know what do to once they retire. They've saved up money, looked forward to having time to do what they wanted, but now that they're actually retired, they are lost and unsure of what to do next. That's part of the reason why you also want to have dreams that evolve as life changes.

When you're 25, you are probably not dreaming about retirement. But when you are 45, it should come into view. Do you have a mental picture (a vision board in your mind) of what your retirement will look like? Do you see yourself traveling and golfing at the finest courses in the world? Perhaps you're dreaming about your next career, maybe real estate. Maybe, like me, you dream of mentoring or doing something philanthropic. Bucket lists (whether you like the term or not) are a collection of dreams you hope to achieve in your lifetime. Whatever you choose, set your goals and start working toward a new dream. And never stop researching and learning along the way.

Life should be about challenging yourself and not standing idle. I post motivational pictures and quotes on Instagram and remind people that if you stay idle, you don't grow. It's like having your car idling instead of moving forward—you'll never get to a destination if you stay still.

Remember, your goals should be both long-term and short-term. You need to reach the short-term goals en route to the long-term goals. If, for example, you are travelling cross-country, you can determine how many hours you can drive per day and how many miles you will cover during those hours. Then you can set places

▲ chapter 5 / dream big

you will reach as smaller goals along the journey, such as stopping in Chicago, in St. Louis, at the Grand Canyon, and so forth. In real estate, it can be getting your real estate license, making your first purchase, making your first sale, reaching one million dollars in sales, reaching ten million, and so forth.

It's also important to acknowledge reaching each goal as an achievement. With each small milestone, take a pause and reward yourself. Too many people have long-term dreams and goals, but they ignore the steps they've taken and goals they've accomplished along the way. By acknowledging these steps, or smaller goals, you continue motivating yourself, plus you enjoy the journey. That's also very important. In my case, those smaller goals are tied to larger ones. For example, I enjoy looking for properties and figuring out how to increase their value. I also love going to car auctions or even spending time online looking at supercars. These activities are what make life so worthwhile and enjoyable. The journey is a major part of it. People who have money land in their lap are obviously thrilled, but they miss the all-important journey. It means so much more when you've taken the journey to reach your dreams—even with the bumps and detours you experience along the way.

A Recipe for Success

Once you know what your passion is and can see your dream clearly in front of you, it's time to get practical experience, and understand that you won't start at the top. You need to do the research on whatever it is you want to achieve and understand exactly what it will take to make your dream come true.

Next, you have two options: you can dream of being an owner or work inside the business. For example, you could own a restaurant or be a chef/owner, you could own a dance studio or also be giving the lessons, you could own a tutoring service or be a tutor who owns such a service. The point is, you can be passionate about being hands on in the field, or about being an entrepreneur and have other people with expertise run the business. Some retail store owners love waiting on customers, while others prefer to do the marketing, crunch the

Achieving a Dream . . . a Success Story

There's a local restaurant that Leyla and I love. It's called Javier's and it's one of the best Mexican restaurants we've ever been to. Over the years, I've become good friends with the owner, Javier Sosa, who shared his story with me.

Javier started cooking in a restaurant at age 13 in Tijuana. Later, he came to America, but he had to start from the bottom as a dishwasher. After about ten years of working the same job, he had very little money but the thing that kept him going was his dream. When he was not washing dishes, he would study different food combinations and try all sorts of recipes on his own. Javier never stopped dreaming, and like so many young chefs, his dream was to have his own restaurant one day.

Finally, after many years of washing dishes, cooking, and waiting on people, Javier and another waiter who worked at the same restaurant decided to open their own restaurant and called it Javier's Cantina.

Javier's Cantina first opened in Laguna Beach in 1995. Within no time, the restaurant was a major success. I remember having to wait in a long line going out the front door. But Javier didn't stop there. About ten years after the first location opened, they opened another restaurant in Newport Coast, and he tells me it is one of the highest grossing restaurants in Southern California. They've since opened three more restaurants, each doing incredibly well.

Javier achieved his dream of becoming a chef and of being a restaurant owner. It took a long time and a lot of hard work . . . plus meeting the right people, which means having a little luck, too.

numbers, and come up with great ideas to expand the business. Either way, you need to learn as much as possible about the business, which means rolling up your sleeves and working in the industry for a while. Most of the best coaches in sports, for example, played the game at some level, and whether they were good at it or not, they learned how the game was played. Those who have really excelled at coaching are those who dug deeper, learned more, and came up with their own ideas and their own strategies. That's what I did with real estate. I spent countless hours immersing myself in how the real estate industry works.

Besides gaining knowledge, immersing yourself in the industry, and working in it gives you the opportunity to meet people along the way who can help you later on. Keep in mind, business is as much about who you know as what you know. Also remember, starting and growing a business takes patience, means learning from your mistakes (and those you see around you), and requires that you keep a positive attitude while focusing on your dreams and your destination.

Keep on Dreaming

People ask me why I still get excited over new opportunities. They tell me I've got enough money to last a lifetime or a couple more generations. The truth is that I love looking for new opportunities in real estate or other ventures. I love the challenge and thinking about new possibilities. And when a dream comes true, it's such a great feeling of achievement and accomplishment. I used to dream about seeing myself in a Ferrari—my first supercar was a red Ferrari, which I bought by working very hard and saving up money every week. I felt great. I had achieved something I had been dreaming about for years.

Today, I dream about having a $100 million car collection and eventually selling it, along with my auto gallery (the building in which the cars reside). I spent close to $1 million on building and remodeling the auto gallery, which needed a lot of tech installed because the city had requirements to meet before they would allow cars to be parked inside. Because the cars have gasoline and oils in them, I needed to equip the building with special computers, carbon monoxide sensors, huge fans and other items to be able to park them indoors. My goal is to keep buying my way up and have about 25 cars worth roughly $4 million each and, who knows, maybe I'll keep dreaming into a billion dollar collection. It's a dream and a challenge. At the end of the day, you need both to ignite your desire to learn more and, in effect, achieve more.

YOUR ROADMAP TO SUCCESS

▶ Don't be afraid to dream big. Be realistic. No, you will not be able to fly, and invisibility is probably not attainable . . . yet.

▶ Make a dream or vision board and write on it as if you're living in that moment today. How are you going to feel living in your dream home, driving that new car, etc.?

▶ Remember, meeting small goals on the road to big dreams is possible. You should always have a destination in mind.

▶ While on the road, keep on doing research and learning. Don't stand still—keep moving forward.

▶ Be accessible so you can meet successful, like-minded people who may be able to help you in some manner. Learn from them as well.

▶ Don't forget to appreciate and enjoy your journey.

▶ Stay the course: Too many people think about quitting before they reach their destination, so be tough with yourself. My attitude is to never give up. Make that your attitude, too.

▶ Think about Javier—he stayed the course and made it. Look at your five- and ten-year goals.

▶ Think about your motivation—I wanted to help my family and become financially independent. What's your motivation? Keep it in front of you as you continue on your destination . . . which is your dream.

6

power up: learning and knowledge

They say knowledge is power, which is why you need to "power up." This does not necessarily mean gaining only classroom or textbook knowledge. This means getting knowledge from experience, trial and error, and staying on top of your industry by using the most valid (and up to date) data and resources you can find. It also means going back and talking to the people you've surrounded yourself with over the years.

They also say curiosity killed the cat, but I say it made the cat a lot smarter. I've always been curious. While I did not get a college education, I got my education from constantly seeking information on the internet, in the media, from anything I read, by talking with other people and asking a lot of questions. Don't accept things as they are; always try to delve deeper and see what else you can learn. I must admit I spend probably two or three hours a night on internet news sites, such as CNBC, Bloomberg, and Yahoo!, until I fall asleep. I do try to get some engagement with my fans as well, but a majority of the time, I'm powering up when the rest of my family is powering down.

To be successful in any field, you need to understand the value of acquiring knowledge. Nobody is born a genius. We all have to learn how to walk, talk, and so forth. We continue to learn throughout all phases of life. To power up means to become a sponge and soak information from all around you day in and day out.

While learning about a broad range of subjects is wonderful and will help you find your passion, at some point you need to start focusing on what is most interesting to you. My wife Leyla, for example, decided to go into the beauty industry because it interested her, it was a passion, and something that became an integral part of her life while appearing in movies and on television. She learned as much as possible about the subject of beauty and hair. Likewise, when I first discovered real estate investing, I was fascinated. It gave me a direction in which to point my inquisitive mind. I wanted to know as much about real estate as possible.

Attention Grabbers

What happens when you really dig into researching potential business opportunities that interest you is that you learn about many things, and one will always stand out and grab your attention. Any number of things can spark your interest. Perhaps it's what someone in your family has been doing. It may be something you read about, learned about from your peers, or from networking or in school. The point is, we become fascinated by one or more areas of interest; it grabs our attention and does not let go—we keep gravitating toward it. For entertainers, it's singing, dancing, or acting. For a chef, it's preparing food. For a teacher, it's the love of learning and educating others.

We then embark on gaining the knowledge we need to succeed in that area. And it doesn't stop when you learn the basics, or even once you've become successful. I still want to know what's going in the real estate markets—it pulls at me, grabs my attention.

Years ago, people used to buy large sets of encyclopedias, which had all sorts of information inside on many different topics. They had one book for each letter of the alphabet. Today, with the internet, encyclopedias are somewhat extinct. But, very few people ever had the time to read through all of them—they would look up what interested them the most and learn about those subjects. And that's what you will find yourself doing, learning as much as possible about the subjects that interest you the most.

Once you know what you want to learn, you have to dive in. If you want to successfully invest in real estate, you will need to start educating yourself on an ongoing basis. You can never learn too much since things are changing all the time, both in the overall economy and in the real estate market. So, you must start learning and keep learning. The more you know, the more credible you will appear to other investors. It's also important to always stay ahead of the curve, which is the hallmark of the contrarian investor, and that's what I am. I will go against the grain because I do not want to be doing what everyone else is doing. But I can only do that by knowing what everyone else is doing. Staying ahead of the curve also lets you see trends and patterns developing in the future. You do that by diversifying your knowledge base.

Many Sources of Knowledge

There are many ways that we learn. You can acquire knowledge in the classroom, and from reading books like my first book, *Manny Khoshbin's Contrarian Playbook* (GeniusWork Publishing, 2011), as well as this book. I've never been a big reader and finding time to read is difficult with a busy schedule. I must admit that I did learn a lot about real estate from watching what other successful investors did around me and by my own trial and errors. If you do have the time, I advise you to look for books or articles written by people who have succeeded in your chosen field who are relevant to the industry today. Some are known as "thought leaders." Listen to what they have to say. Keep two things in mind as you learn:

1. Every industry goes through changes, so the best book from 1992 will probably not be as accurate or helpful as something that has come out in recent years.

2. Don't believe everything you read. There is a glut of information out there, some of which will be contradictory. People have their own ideas and opinions. They may differ, so find the ones that resonate with you. Also, double check facts and figures.

You can also learn a lot from the media. Early in my career, I became fascinated with the financial media. I read and watched several sources that report on money and the markets. Even though I don't have a lot of stock market activity, I always care about the economy and want to find out what's happening, whether it's the unemployment rate or the ten-year bond yield, which is super key to real estate. Why? When the cost of money goes up, so does the cost of real estate. It's also very important to know when banks are going to raise or lower their spreads, which is the difference between the index your loan is tied to and the rate the bank charges you, it's their margin. For example, between 2006 and 2007, banks were charging as low as 80 basis points over the index because they saw real estate as low risk. Between 2008 and 2011, this spread had ballooned to as much as 300 basis points.

Then of course, there's the internet, where I spend *a lot* of my time. You can learn a great deal from the internet, although you must find reputable websites. Once you find websites that you deem trustworthy, you can benefit by spending a lot of time on them. For example, I have found that www.LoopNet.com and other websites, such as www. CoStar.com, have been very instrumental in my success. Unlike the traditional MLS (Multiple Listing Service), which you need to have a real estate license to use and are mainly for residential properties, LoopNet is a web portal that is open to the public that focuses on commercial property sales and leasing. In some ways it's like Craigslist for real estate. However, to get the most recent listings, you need to become a premium member. Once you find listings that interest you, it's up to you to do your due diligence; explore the submarket's demographic, economic, and census reports to see if population and economy output is in an uptrend or downtrend. For example, you want to buy in a city with a steadily increasing population, well-diversified economy, and an above-average median household income. Take it from me, I learned my lesson the hard way. Years ago, I bought a retail center in Pennsylvania. It was newer construction, very attractive, finished, and priced at $20 per square foot. I saw it online and bought it without researching the city first. I had a hard time leasing the vacancies and learned later that the population of the area had been in steady decline for years. I ended up auctioning off the property. So, learn a lesson from my misstep: whether you are buying property or choosing a new location for your next venture (no matter what business you're in), do your homework on the area and know your criteria.

You can also use offline research to find out more about your industry and the competitive landscape. For example, in real estate, I research the neighborhoods, the buildings, the prices in the area, and the number of buildings sold in a certain amount of time, whether it's the past month, the past six months, or the past year.

Over time, it became easy for me to gauge the value of a property by doing such comparisons for the same type of property. For example, if I see a multi-tenant office building in a certain city, I'll look at similar sized multi-tenant office buildings in that city to see what sellers were asking for them, whether the property was for sale or for lease, and how long it took to lease or sell. I then research how much they were leased or sold for (FYI, some of this information is fee-based). Then, I make sure it fits with my own criteria:

1. Must be a multi-tenant building
2. No more than 30 percent occupied by any single tenant
3. Good location
4. Selling at a discount to replacement cost
5. Has a value add, such as managed poorly, hasn't been maintained, etc.

During the Great Recession, I'd offer sellers an all-cash offer with a short closing. Out of ten such properties, I'd usually find one seller or bank that would entertain my offer. It's always a numbers game. Today, I focus on much larger assets with a minimum of $10 million and up, but still with the same criteria.

I should also mention that I have always done my own research in addition to finding third-party reports. I do this because it lets me

Go for the Personal Touch

When doing offline research, seek out people you can speak to directly. If there is a seminar or an expert in the field doing a speaking engagement, try not just to attend but ask questions and be engaged—and go one step further by talking to the presenter after the event. Compliment them on their presentation, ask questions, and get his or her business card. Meeting people face to face still counts for a lot even in an age of emails and texts. I find it to be a more significant experience.

spring into action quickly rather than waiting for others to give me the information, and I know I can trust the integrity of the data. Today, there are lots of reputable online sources on the economy and on real estate. Find four or five such sites you like that pertain to your own industry and check on them regularly. Once you've done your due diligence, you can focus on how best to network online. And, of course, social media is the best place to start.

Social Media

Social media is a great place to network, especially on a business-oriented site like www.LinkedIn.com, where you can find other professionals discussing business, and you can follow top business people like Richard Branson, Michael Bloomberg, and many others. Since the world has embraced social media in the past several years, you need to keep up with the trends, and this is one source that isn't going away.

Of course, you have to use discretion on social media. As I often say, the good, the bad, and the ugly all come together on the internet. Some people post good information, others are bogus, and some will lead you down the wrong path. Therefore, it's vital that you take nothing on the internet at face value, especially on social media where anyone can play any role. You have to screen people to find out whether or not they are who they say they are. Check their profile on LinkedIn, Google them, and look for articles or interviews about them. A lot of people approach me on social media. Frequently I'll hear from someone who tells me they are a broker and they have a great deal, but nine times out of ten, they are not actually the broker but someone who works for the broker or simply knows a broker. A lot of people are just trying to swim—so doing some due diligence is imperative.

One thing you will learn over time as you deal with more people online, by phone, or in person is when to recognize a red flag. For example, if someone is a fast talker and it all sounds too good to be true, it probably isn't real. Or, if someone says, "Nobody knows about this offer. I'm only giving it to you," that's also a red flag. Then there are people who will tell you they don't want anything for their efforts; they just want to be part of the deal. Again, you should put up the red flag. People don't do things for free. I've had situations in which I plan to meet someone and then when they show up, they are with three other people who have a totally different agenda. It's okay to turn people down, especially once you've gained a reputation. You

Get Licensed!

If your dream is of going into a field where licensing will help you get ahead, definitely get licensed. In some cases, even if you only plan to invest, you might benefit from being licensed. For instance, if you are looking to open your own gym, you may have more credibility and access to buying the best equipment by becoming a licensed personal trainer, even if you do not want to have your own clients. In real estate, for example, you have to be licensed. Even if you are just going to invest in real estate, I strongly recommend you get your real estate license. It's not hard to obtain and costs less than $300 in most states. As a real estate agent, you have access to all the multiple listings. You can start to look at comparable sales in the areas where you hope to be investing and educate yourself. I'm always looking for potential opportunities. I have a very curious mind. Being thirsty for knowledge in the field is important. If you're not constantly learning, you will fall behind.

do not want to be arrogant or rude, but you only have so much time, so you need to be discerning. Time is money, and too many people want your time with no money in sight. Don't let them steal away time that is yours.

Follow the Markets

All businesses, especially real estate, are based on some financial indicators, which means you need to follow numbers and patterns carefully and act, or react, accordingly. Some of the key indicators I follow are: rising interest rates, inflation, unemployment, retail and

Look for Out-of-Step Markets

They say a "rising tide lifts all boats," meaning that improvements in the general economy will benefit all participants in that economy, and vice-versa for a low tide. The truth is, that's not always the case. Sometimes local economic or geographic trends do not mirror the general economy.

In some cases, such as in real estate, you will find local markets that are out of step with the national markets. This was how I ended up investing in properties in places like Arizona and Texas where markets were struggling and I was able to find good deals. Many states, or even cities, are focused on one industry like Houston with oil and gas. Just a few years ago the price of oil was at $25 a barrel. Even though the economy was doing well, they were getting crushed. More recently, Denver has been doing particularly well because of the exploration of natural gas and even the sale of marijuana. Every area is different, so you need to look more closely for local trends. Then, try to estimate how those trends will affect your ability to sell your product, invest your money, and get a decent ROI (return on investment) for the long run. Regardless of your business, it's important to note that local economic or geographic trends do not always mirror the national economy as a whole. You can find good deals and make sales of your product or service in local markets that are out of step with national markets. Listen to the heartbeat of your community.

restaurant sales for some of the biggest chains, and where people invest based on emotions. In other words, I rely on data.

Too many people let their emotions play a factor in their decision making, or they invest based on speculation, which is when you put down a lot of money based on something that will happen in the future. Then, three years later when the market goes bad, you lose your money. That's not investing, that's pure speculation. I avoid speculating; it's too risky.

I've been fortunate that I've become fairly good at timing the market. It's been one of the biggest factors of my success and is something I've learned over the years, but it's not easy, especially when things move quickly as they do today. As a contrarian, I buy when most people sell, and I've made most of my wealth buying distressed real estate during recessions. Buy into the fear! It's similar to the stock market in periods of volatility—if you can go back 100 years, you can see almost all of the major pullbacks in the stock market had high volatility. One indicator I follow consistently is VIX (the Volatility Index, or fear factor). The higher the VIX trades, the more fear is in the market. That tells me people are acting with high emotions and in short sight. That is my cue to go bold. Think about the market indicators in your own industry. When do they tell you to go big?

Are You Bold Enough?

I must admit that a lot of credit for my success comes from having the guts to pull the trigger. It also comes from knowing when not to pull the trigger. Most people don't act at the right time. First, they jump into the stock market too late when it's at the top—then it starts going down, and they sell too late. Others may jump into business ventures when a business or industry is over-saturated. I take calculated risks. When I made my first million-dollar deal on a vacant, abandoned shopping center, I bought it and made the deal in six months. I put $67,000 down and got an SBA loan for the rest. It was a unique situation and a gutsy move, but it worked. It's always difficult when you don't know what's going to happen. When a market has been a sellers' market (where sellers have the upper hand) for multiple years and then you hear this is the best time to buy real estate, that's when I sell and wait for the cycle to change to a buyers' market. I always like to go against the herd, which is why I consider myself a contrarian. If you are very knowledgeable in your industry you can also become a contrarian—but that can take time. Too many people take a single course or read a book or even an article and are ready to jump into investing or buying a business. It takes a lot more knowledge than that. Not that we won't all make some mistakes, but jumping the gun and assuming you are an instant expert is one mistake you should avoid. Remember, it's important to know when you should act on an opportunity and when you should hold off. Timing is key to your success.

You've Got to Act Fast

Did you ever plan to go to a show with friends, but by the time you got everyone on board, the show was sold out? The same can happen with deals—the longer it takes to get your ducks in a row, the more likely someone will beat you to it. You need to make a quick evaluation of the situation and then think like an ER doctor and act fast—there's no time to wait.

In 2008, a broker friend called me and said, "You have to come now, meet me at this property, and bring your checkbook!" I trusted his judgment, so I did. It was an ocean view home that a bank was going to auction and had just dropped in price from $8 million to $6 million! There were about three other agents with their buyers previewing the home. I was shocked at the value and loved the location. In fact, it was the neighborhood I dreamed of living in, so I was waiting for such a deal. I immediately wrote an all-cash offer of the full price with a $250,000 non-refundable deposit. There were over ten offers on the property by the weekend, but mine was the only non-contingent, all-cash offer with a quick close. So, the bank accepted mine, but continued accepting backup offers as high as $6.7 million. I ended up living in this house for ten years and starting my family there. I just sold it in 2017 for $3 million more than the original purchase price.

This example goes to show that the ability to act fast is vital to success. This is true when investing in real estate, buying your own home, starting a business, or purchasing a stock. If you wait to buy the house or start the business, someone will get there ahead of you, and if you wait to buy the stock, the price can go up before you have a chance

Manny the Negotiator
Morteza Hajian, Investor and Friend

Manny is very motivated. When people are around Manny, they also get motivated. He just has that kind of personality.

I remember when I invested with Manny in properties in Houston. We were making good money and collecting good rent, but Manny kept telling us that it was not going to stay like that forever. The prices were going to drop and it was going to go down the drain. So, when Manny decided to sell and get out, we did the same. This was maybe eight months before the market crashed in 2008. When he closed, it was about four months before everything went south. I remember that he told us if we had stayed we would have lost our shirts. He was right. He's not only very bright but he can see the future very clearly. He stays on top of things; that's why he's so successful.

Manny's also a good negotiator. I recall that we were negotiating with a tough client from Asia. The negotiations over the lease went on for two months. I was learning from watching him negotiate, but I called him and told him I didn't have the patience for such a negotiation. He told me to just give him a little more time. He was frustrated like I was, but he could handle it; even when it was tough, he could handle it. Finally, he signed the contract and later sold the building for a profit. He was incredibly patient; he just kept at it. Nobody else I know could have done this.

Manny is excellent at negotiating leases and buying the property. He's also very sharp when it comes to numbers. When someone gives him the numbers, he calculates it all in his head and tells you how much the building is worth, how much we're going to spend, and how much we could make. Whatever it is, he just calculates it. Then you go back and put it all on a spreadsheet and the numbers come out just like he said they would. I'm telling you, the guy's a genius.

to jump in. A friend of mine calls me the Indiana Jones of real estate investing because I recognize the value of making bold decisions at the right time without being reckless. Indiana Jones couldn't stand around waiting for things to happen or he would have been killed many times in his films. I've learned that this is what separates the most successful investors from the rest of the pack. You need to be bold and seize opportunity quickly.

Don't let fears stop you. Don't let yourself think, "I'm not ready," or "The market will go lower," or "I'll find a better deal." In fact, most of the times I bought my best assets were times I wasn't ready with cash, but I knew I had a bargain and could find the resources to bridge the gap. When it comes to investing quickly, take charge—relying on other people will slow you down. Also knowing your criteria lets you move forward immediately because you know what you do and do not want to buy. You also need to have the funds readily available or have the resources in some manner. Knowledge, research, and preparation are vital, but without the ability to act quickly, you will usually lose out to someone who acted fast.

I do not want to be the investor who waits and waits and waits before making a decision while doing too much due diligence. I've seen investors lose wonderful opportunities because they experience analysis paralysis, meaning they don't make a move because they are stuck overanalyzing the deal. By the time they are ready to buy, it has been sold. Or, by the time they figure out when to sell, the buyers have found better deals. Your own sense of timing is important, and what Kenny Rogers sang in his song "The Gambler," is so true when it comes to investing: "You've got to know when to hold 'em, know when to fold 'em." The difference between gambling and investing is that gambling is essentially playing a game of chance. Investing is looking at a number of factors and taking an educated, calculated risk.

Trial and Error

When it comes to learning, one of the most common ways we learn, in general, is through trial and error. I must have had about

15 failed businesses over the years and many experiences within each of them. Don't be afraid to fail. I learned a lot from each failed business. In fact, while starting out, I often learned it was not the right business for me. In real estate, I've learned a lot through the process of making deals—good ones and bad ones. In fact, you can learn more from your mistakes than from your successes. From day one, you need to tell yourself that it is OK to fail and to make mistakes. You also get closer to what you want by continuing to try again and again. It's said that Thomas Edison tried nearly 1,000 times to invent the light bulb before he had that "light bulb" moment—literally. Had he given up because he kept failing, we'd all be in the dark today.

When you make a mistake, you need to ask yourself how you can do better—you've got to focus in on the mistake and understand what went wrong. Perhaps you didn't do enough due diligence. Perhaps you did not know when it was time to get out of a bad deal. Too many people stubbornly try to make it work and lose more money and more time when they could be using that same time and money to find and get in on a better investment. You need to know when it's better to just walk away. Sometimes you can change a situation and make it work, but other times you can't. If you stop the bleeding, you come out ahead because you free yourself to look for better opportunities. By staying in bad investments, you are just allowing yourself to lose on another opportunity!

It's OK to lose money—I've lost money on maybe six of the 100 or so deals I've made; that's not a bad percentage. It happens. If I had stayed in those deals, I would have lost a lot more money and early on in my career, I might have even gone bankrupt. You're not going to build your empire by throwing good money after bad money in losing propositions. Too many people are scared of losing and it becomes all about their ego. They can't accept a loss, so they hang on and keep on losing. Playing it safe is fine, but the most successful people take some risks—the key is to take calculated ones where you are following trends and staying on top of the movements of the market. Remember, it's not an exact science.

Lessons Learned

Knowledge is always a must when embarking on your journey no matter what your goal is in the end. From gaining knowledge, you can set criteria for yourself in the future. In every industry there are tricks of the trade—you'll learn them in many different ways. For example, in real estate you should never buy a single tenant building because if they leave, you have nobody paying rent. I learned this the hard way—I remember losing $5 million because the tenant in a building I owned, Boeing Commercial Airplanes, failed to get a major contract with NASA, so they vacated, and I was left holding the bag. I learned that it would cost a lot to turn the property into a multi-tenant building with more bathrooms, common space, and so forth. I also learned that it is better to get out and take your losses than to lose more money on a bad business deal or investment.

As I mentioned earlier, you also need to take calculated risks in any investment or business venture. For example, in real estate I look at price per square foot. I never buy a property over replacement cost, so if a building is priced at $300 per square foot, I would need a 30 to 40 percent discount of $200 per square foot. If not, you can't be competitive. If you're looking at a ten-year-old building at $300 per square foot up against a brand new building at $300 per square foot, you're already in the red because properties depreciate. I consider the depreciation.

The other important thing I learned from my years in real estate is how important the age-old real estate saying, "Location, location, location," really is. If the property is next to a freeway or surrounded by empty buildings, you're best steering clear. You also want to consider curb appeal and the energy that you get from the property. This applies to so many businesses. The wrong location or neighborhood can be a disaster to a retail business, restaurant, or medical facility.

These are a few of the lessons I've learned as I powered up along the journey. Think about how you can expand your knowledge base in your own industry. What are steps you can take right now to help create your customized road map?

YOUR ROADMAP TO SUCCESS

▶ Failure is your friend, not your enemy. You can learn more from your failures than your successes. Get comfortable with failure.

▶ Recognize when it's best to walk away.

▶ It's OK to lose money. Too many make money all about their ego—especially when they are losing it.

▶ The more you focus on education, the more you will:

  – Build confidence in your decision making abilities.

  – See patterns and, over time, be better able to read the different markets.

  – Take calculated risks.

  – Be able to act fast.

  – Learn from your mistakes.

▶ If you are passionate about something, as I am about real estate and cars, you will find that you really enjoy educating yourself.

7

balancing your life

People ask me how I find time to take care of my many business deals, spend time with Leyla, be with my kids, and enjoy my hobby, which is, of course, my car collection. What many people don't know is that I'm spread out even more than that. In this chapter, I'll explain my balancing act and offer my take on how to manage yours—just remember that there is no one-size-fits-all solution to juggling work, family, and everything else.

Balancing your life is kind of like one of those acrobatic acts where people are standing on top of one another balancing themselves, or like the pyramid formed by cheerleading squads. It's like each person on the pyramid represents another important part of your life. You want to keep them all up there without anyone falling. Not so easy, is it?

To really appreciate and enjoy what you have, balancing the many aspects of your life is essential . . . and many people aren't very good at it. I was one of those people in my first marriage. I was wrapped up in my business and not spending enough time and energy on my marriage. In the end, the marriage blew up.

I admit, it's hard to say no to business when it comes knocking at your door, especially when you're selling real estate and qualified buyers don't come along every day. However, if you don't know when to put the brakes on and slow down, you may find yourself out of control and missing out on a lot of your life or you may simply get burnt out. Many people get a taste of success and they want to scale it, so they just dive into it 24/7. The next thing they know, ten years have gone by and they've built a huge empire but lost sight of everything else. Then, when they finally come up for air, they realize that their spouse is now their ex, their kids are now teenagers, other family members, as well as friends, have moved on, and they've missed so much of their personal life that not even money can buy it back.

So, how do you balance work, family, and everything else? For one thing, you need to accept that you have to make many compromises, have a positive attitude, and know that it can be done, even in marriages in which partners work together.

Balancing Businesses

Besides running my own business, Leyla and I, as mentioned earlier, are partners in her business. Warning: This type of arrangement will not work for all couples, but it can work well, provided you clarify your positions and respect each other's roles. For example, a couple from China, Andrew and Peggy Cherng, launched Panda Inn in 1973 and Panda Express in 1983, which now has 2,000 locations. They made it work and reaped the benefits. Going back even further, Doris and Don Fisher teamed up to open The Gap way back in 1969. Then, of course, there's the incredibly successful philanthropic foundation run by Bill and Melinda Gates. Yes, husbands and wives can work together . . . but it takes some effort.

The trick is knowing how to combine, and then separate, business and marriage. For example, Leyla and I sometimes have to go to Los Angeles for meetings or to an expo or a beauty show in Las Vegas. We take the opportunity to make a full weekend out of it, working at the

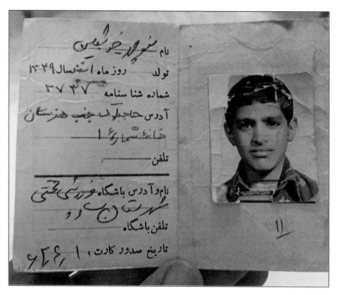

My fighting spirit began long before I came to the U.S.
This is my karate score card from 35 years ago when we
still lived in Iran!

When I was about 14 years old I bought these dumbbells
for $2 at a garage sale. Exercise has always helped
power me through.

Me and my dad in Arizona when I was 15. He risked it all for us to come to America, and risked even more so we could stay.

My parents at their friends video rental store in Costa Mesa, California around 1986.

Here, I'm 16 or 17 in my bedroom office. I thought I was a big businessman with a RadioShack PC and bunch of floppy disks. They made me feel official.

Time flies! This is how I kept track of my door-to-door nut sales business 29 years ago.

Making it official. Here's my very first office at age 18.

Years later, I've upgraded my office and have my dream cars in view instead of on posters.

Fun fact: This is the car from the poster in my first office. I rented it for prom during my senior year of high school.

Before and after: The car that we had to live in and the car I'm driving today. It's been 29 years and I'm still working hard every day.

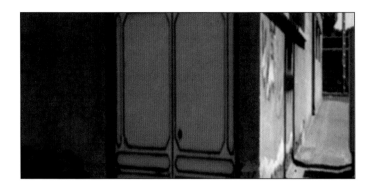

Before and after: My childhood home in Saveh, Iran, and in my home today in Newport Beach, California.

My car collection has grown over the years!

Mr. Koenigsegg surprised me with a 24-karat gold carbon fiber helmet to match my Phoenix [car] at the Cars N Copters 2018 event in Huntington Beach, California.

I flew to France to meet with the Hermès design team to customize my Pagani Hermès Edition. Experience of a lifetime!

Here's Leyla with the Pagani Hermès. Dream car and dream wife.

Did I mention we got married? Here's a pic from our wedding day.

Leyla and I are grateful to be able to give back to the community. Here we are at the Orangewood Foundation Gala.

Priscilla, Enzo, and me. They make it all worthwhile.

The Khoshbins!

We're a car family. Priscilla and I are decked out in Koenigsegg and Pagani.

Three generations of Khoshbins. Thankful to my dad who had the courage to leave it all behind and bring us to this great country.

The road from Iran was long with many twists and turns, but the destination was worth the journey. And now, our journey continues.

Here I am enjoying a cigar at The Cubano Room.

Never look back. Always look forward. Keep pushing.
Keep driving!

event and then going to the casino to gamble, or somewhere on the strip to see a show, or to a club for dancing. It works well because we have a planned work schedule and time to step away from business and enjoy ourselves. At home, we plan to have date nights at least once a week, even if we're tired and all we do is grab a quick dinner and then come back home. It's important to break the routine and put business aside. On weekends, Leyla's business is closed and I do not work, although I do check in on my laptop for about an hour, but we spend the rest of the time with our kids. We try to make time for each of our top priorities: our family, each other, and our work. Remember, there are only 24 hours in a day, so you need to find time for all of the things you love, which means dividing up your time carefully.

In our case, we have our own businesses, I have my own companies and Leyla runs two companies, which I'm a part of. In her businesses, she runs the show and knows far more than I do about the beauty and hair industry, but I join her for meetings, go with her on some business trips, and discuss deals. I know numbers, and she knows product development, design, and what her target audience wants to buy.

Unfortunately, when you're working together and discussing, or sometimes arguing, about business during the day, it's difficult to switch gears when you get home and shift into husband-and-wife mode. We try to be careful to stop ourselves without letting the day spill over into our personal life together. I'll admit, however, that it does take some practice, learning how to turn the switch off before you leave the office to go home. At first, it's super difficult and you'll need some practice, but in time it gets easier. You will need to set some rules together and then make sure you're both on board with those rules.

To make it more challenging, our individual offices are in the same building that I purchased in 2011. This lets us meet for lunch and talk business and not have to talk about it again when we get home. However, on the days we do not have time to meet for lunch, we do what most couples who don't see each other all day do—we talk about work a little at home. I'll get home and start telling her about some of my day, and then she'll tell me about her day, and then before we know it, we're busy with the kids. Some nights are interrupted by phone calls; Leyla's on her phone dealing with a business issue, and I'm on my phone dealing with a tenant issue. After that, we're too tired to catch up so we just call it a day. Finding some time to sleep is also part of a balanced day—and night. And for us, part of balancing our days and nights also includes focusing on helping others.

Philanthropy

Giving something back is so important. It's something you definitely want to make time for. Leyla and I do engage in philanthropic activities, which I will discuss in greater detail in the final chapter of the book. We go to charity events, often for Children's Hospital of Orange County (CHOC). We've been involved with them for five years, and Leyla is now on the committee.

Meanwhile, I'm one of ambassadors of Talk About Curing Autism (TACA), which I've been involved with for ten years. Interestingly, I got involved because a buddy of mine, a professional poker player, was coming down to visit me and told me he had a poker gig for a charity. He invited me to go with him, so I went and heard a speech by the founder of the organization that really touched me. It was a small organization in Orange County, and I thought that since it's a great cause for kids, I would get involved in some manner. That was in 2007, and I've been going back to the poker event and contributing to them ever since. I've donated a lot of money and given a lot of silent auction items. For example, I've given away a weekend getaway with a Rolls-Royce and a chauffeur to drive the winners around. I've also given away one-year memberships at my cigar lounge, which is roughly a $10,000 membership, in addition to donating money. I enjoy doing something for them because it benefits children.

Getting involved in charitable work is a great way to take the focus away from yourself, your business, and anything else that may be stressful. It lets you focus on what others are going through and how they are coping with their lives. It's a great way to put things into perspective. I encourage people to add this to their activities and find a little time to put philanthropy into their balancing act. It keeps you humble, and it's very fulfilling.

Hobbies and Passions: Cars and Cigars

You also need time for your hobbies. Ever since I was a teenager, I've loved exotic cars. I bought my first exotic car in 1992, a Nissan 300ZX Twin Turbo. Fast-forward ten years, and I had moved to Corona del Mar where my neighbor owned an exotic car dealership and always had Ferraris parked outside of his house. He also drove one around. Watching him, I started falling in love with Ferraris as well as Porsches. As a result, my first real supercar was a 1992 Ferrari F40, which I purchased in 2005 and is highly revered by car collectors. I have since continued collecting rare supercars, which are my real passion and joy. Currently, my collections consist of two Bugatti Veyrons, five McLarens one of which is a special McLaren P1™, three Porsches including a Porsche Carrera GT, three Rolls-Royces, a Koenigsegg Agera RS Special Edition called Phoenix, and a Pagani Huayra Hermès Edition 1/1, which is really the jewel and the pride of my collection.

I commissioned Hermès, a French luxury goods manufacturer founded in 1837, and maker of fine leather bags, to design and do the entire interior of my Pagani, which is an amazing, hand-built Italian supercar. Only 100 Huayra coupes were made, and mine is uniquely a creation of Hermès and Pagani. It took me 18 months, and several trips to Paris and Italy, to meet with designers from both luxury brands, but it was an amazing once-in-a-lifetime experience! I have a car with a Hermès leather interior—and a matching set of luggage (honest!). I am now working with Hermès on a second car, a Bugatti Chiron.

I also love going to car shows and auctions. In fact, I go to Monterey every August for a few days during their annual car week where they have car shows and rallies as well as car auctions in nearby Pebble Beach. It's great to be surrounded by all sorts of classic cars. Sometimes I bid on a few, but I don't chase them. It's more about having fun, seeing what's there, and then trying to land a good deal.

Even though they are a hobby, I always have an entrepreneurial spirit when it comes to my passion for cars. In fact, I view them in a similar way that I do great pieces of property—though I'd prefer to keep them than sell to the highest bidder. To me, they're like works of art. Just as many people invest in art because it's their passion, they are also mindful of the investment aspect. Similarly, when I look at cars as art, I also view them as investments, knowing that they are of great value, except for the Rolls-Royces, which are losing money while the others are becoming more valuable. The difference is that the Rolls-Royces, besides being cars that I have driven often, are not as rare as the other cars. As is the case with my real estate investments, I bought many of the cars during the recession when people were selling off some of their assets.

Cars aren't my only passion, though. It's important to have some passions that you can enjoy away from work, from family, and from everything else. You also want some alone time. For example, I also own a cigar lounge (www.CubanoRoom.com) where I can go to relax by myself or meet another successful member while smoking a fine cigar.

I treat my passions like a business because that's who I am so I can enjoy them and also make money; but it doesn't have to be that way. If you enjoy bicycling, you don't have to go and open a bicycle store. You can simply find a group of riders, do some travelling, and have fun. It's important to fit some alone time into your busy balancing act. We all need some moments when we escape from everyone and everything. The best thing to do is figure out what makes you happy and balance the hustle of your busy life with your own passion. It's important because otherwise you get burnt out and end up a grumpy old man or woman.

Extended Family

Family time is so important to me, both as a father and as a member of an extended family. Besides spending time with Leyla and my children, I see my parents often. I bought them a ranch about 90 miles away from Newport Beach back in 2004. Now they visit us every Friday or Saturday—they come down, and we have a barbecue and play backgammon or cards. However, now that my dad is over 70, and has some physical issues, and my mom is in her early 70s as well, the ranch is getting a little too hard for them to manage. Therefore, I'm going to find them a place closer to where we are living. I want them to be able to see their grandchildren often and not have to travel 90 minutes each time they want to visit.

We also see Leyla's mom and sister. Her mom, at nearly 60, still works as a registered nurse and lives in Beverly Hills. Leyla's sister is also nearby in San Diego where she works for a company called Houzz, an online community for home construction, landscape design, home improvement, repairs, and so forth.

Leyla and I both recognize the importance of having our extended family nearby and making time to spend together. We know how important it is for them to see their grandchildren. Otherwise, time goes by quickly, and you suddenly realize that it's been years since you spent some quality time together.

Perspectives on Balance

Leyla and I share common perspectives on balance. When I asked her what she thought our challenges were, she said, "When it comes to balancing our life together, I find it's one of our challenges. There's not really a lot of balance right now, especially because we have two little ones, and we're kind of in the thick of it all. We're not getting very good sleep. On any given night, one of the kids gets up and needs us, so we're not at our optimal best right now."

"I just started working out to take care of myself. When you're a mom, you can forget about yourself, so I'm trying to focus a little more attention on myself so I can be a better mom and a better wife," explains Leyla, who also points out that in many ways we are a lot alike, which is so important in a marriage. It helps to have similar perspectives, similar ideas, and similar values. We are both driven in our careers but also very devoted to family, which is why neither of us works on the weekends—it's one way that we make family time a priority.

"Being a lot alike is very good in many ways," notes Leyla since we have so much in common. Yet, she adds, "it can also be bad because neither of us balances the other in certain areas. For example, we are both impatient, sometimes stubborn, and we are both control freaks. We don't balance each other out in those regards. Yet there's more good than bad and for the most part we find it beneficial to have a lot in common," explains Leyla.

One thing that Leyla and I both believe can help us balance our lives more easily is learning to delegate. "That's our biggest goal: to delegate different parts of our business. We need to find qualified people that we trust so that we can have more time to be with our family and to travel more so we don't feel like our hands are tied," says Leyla.

I agree completely—we both have a hard time delegating. This is not uncommon when it comes to business owners. As entrepreneurs, we tend to get so busy working in the business and feeling that if we don't do everything it won't get done. The problem is if you let yourself get too deep in all the little details, you end up not controlling the business, but letting the business control you. As a result, you never get the time to spend with your family or do other things you enjoy. It is very hard for either of us to let go. I was on my own trying to build my businesses for so long that I'm used to doing everything myself. But, I think Leyla and I will start learning how to delegate, at least when it comes to some of the chores, like going through my 45,000 unread emails.

It's not easy because, as Leyla says, we are a lot alike. We both have the entrepreneurial spirit and like calling the shots, making the plans, and then executing them, but we both need to find a way to step back a little so we can do more family activities. It's also better for business. Delegating means that while other people are doing some of the tasks, you can spend your time making bigger decisions and looking at ways to grow, to find new products or properties, or to reshape the business.

"Sometimes we look at each other, and I know we're both thinking, *What are we doing? We used to be so much more fun*," says Leyla. "Now there are days when we come home and we're so spent that we just want to crash on the bed and do nothing . . . we have a lot of those days," adds Leyla with a laugh.

Slow Down and Make Some Rules for Yourself

In the end, the best way to balance your life may be to try slowing down a little. Stephen Covey, who wrote the popular book *The 7 Habits of Highly Effective People* (Free Press, 2004), says, "Most of us spend too much time on what is urgent and not enough time on what is important." Considering how many people spend a lot of time every day at work putting out fires, Covey may be right. After you've been in business for a while you learn that everything is not an emergency. In fact, patience has helped me become successful, waiting for the right times to buy and the right times to sell. I don't panic and react when everyone else does—remember, I'm a contrarian.

By slowing down a little, you can take time to make the right decisions. You can even stop and take a moment to say "no." I find that sometimes I just cannot take on another responsibility and have to say no. It's OK. Neither Leyla nor I can handle all of the things requested of us. You can do the same—say "no" if you feel you are being stretched too thin and cannot afford to divide your time up any more. Remember, there are only 24 hours in a day. After seven hours of sleep (we don't get that very often with two young children), you need to divide up your waking hours into business, family time, and everything else.

Therefore, you not only need to set some rules, but you need to stick to them as much as possible. For example, if someone calls me about setting up a meeting on the weekend, I politely remind them about my rule not to do work on weekends unless it's a major emergency—then we can set a time to meet during the week. Another example of one of my self-sustaining rules is all about how to retain your agency and identity. And, yes, your money, too. Surprisingly, I've found that this rule overlaps a few areas of life, and you can apply it broadly.

My "Solo Investing" Rule

I now stick to a rule that I will not take on other investors. Instead, I fly solo. This goes back to balancing your life. You need to decide what you can and cannot make time for. It's not that I don't like helping friends, family, and other investors that I know. It's just that sometimes it requires time and effort that I don't always have and headaches that I'd prefer to avoid. That's why people warn you not to invest other people's money unless it's your job.

I started investing on my own, with my own money. Then, around 2005, a lot of my friends, along with friends of friends started saying, "You're making so much money, you're doing great, you're buying Ferraris, driving a Rolls-Royce, and own high-rise buildings. Why don't you share the wealth?" So, I thought, why not bring them in. There were about ten people, including both friends and family, that came in with me and invested. But as much as I liked these people and wanted them to do well, I found that I had to do a lot of babysitting. Investing takes time and patience. People would be emailing me constantly asking things like why I had not yet doubled their money or how much they could make. And often they had very high expectations.

It's funny how they wanted to get into business with me, but when I asked them for a management fee to pay for the extra time I was putting in, they complained. I'd hear things like, "You're worth $100 million and drive a Rolls-Royce, and you're charging me a fee?" I would tell them, "It's a business deal, I want to do everything properly, and I'm spending my time on the property."

Over time, I found it to be too much of a headache and went back to doing my own investing. The truth is, while your intention is to help people, when you're dealing with money, it can also become a liability. This is because when you take somebody's money for an investment, and you have fiduciary responsibilities, you become a partner and have to answer to them. Overall, they were happy, but in this case, it was becoming a headache largely because of one investor/partner. In any group of people, whether they are working for you or investing, there will usually be one bad apple that makes everything more difficult. In this case, I had one partner who was emailing everybody in the group and questioning my fee and asking me why this property didn't go up as much as he had expected or as much as I said it could go up. The answer is simple. Investing is not an exact science. I was doing the best that I could, and my intentions were always good. I was not out to screw anybody—that's not who I am.

I had one unfortunate situation in which I helped someone make a lot of money, but when they reinvested a large portion of it in another venture of mine, they lost a lot of their investment. They were very upset with me, but I could not guarantee them, or anyone else, that a deal is foolproof. I have a tremendous track record of success, but it's not perfect. No investor can guarantee success every time. In the end, they still made money on their initial investment but not as much as they had hoped for, and it cost us a friendship.

This doesn't mean that I don't think real estate is a great means of making a lot of money. Not only have I had success, but so many successful people before me have made their mark in real estate. It's the basis of the most wealthy in the history of mankind—you look at the Rothschild family, you look at the idea of owning and selling land that will always be there. That's why you're called a landlord: you are lord of the land—it's very powerful.

As long as you have the principles right, buy low, sell high, be patient and remember location, location, location you usually can't lose buying real estate. You just need to remember, it's cyclical like most markets, and you need to be able to weather the storm during recessions.

Me Time!

You need "me" time to regroup mentally by giving yourself some time to relax and unwind. I relax and unwind at my cigar club or take one of my supercars out for a drive with a few other friends. Where do you relax and unwind? For many people it's on the golf course, while for some it's on a sailboat or in a yoga class. Find your place for alone time and do what you enjoy. Bill Gates finds the time to read 50 books a year, LinkedIn CEO Jeff Weiner schedules two hours a day for thinking time, and Spanx inventor Sara Blakely spends her alone time writing in her journals. "Me" time isn't about being selfish—it's about staying sane.

The goal of a balanced life is to feel good not only about your business but also about your family, extended family, your hobbies, your charitable work, and your "me" time. If you can find the time to do all of these things, plus some exercise to keep your mind and body fit, you have achieved a balanced life. But remember, as Leyla says, "it's not easy, and we're still working at it."

When you're young you may be focused on one and only one goal, but as you grow and your life expands, more things will matter in your life. If you don't recognize all of your needs and try hard to include and balance the different aspects of your life, you will likely have some regrets.

Keep in mind that being rich in life doesn't always refer to having the most money but instead refers to getting the most *out* of life. That comes from finding your balance.

 YOUR ROADMAP TO SUCCESS

► First you need to prioritize what is important to you. Decide what you can and cannot make time for in your business and your life.

► Then you need to make time for each activity that matters:

  – Work and family (or family and work) are the top priorities for most people.

  – Friends, hobbies, and extended family should all be in the mix.

  – Exercise is a must to fit into your schedule; there are plenty of options.

  – You should also make time to give something back.

► Invest wisely. Your business needs to be able to weather the storm in any economic climate, including recession.

► Prioritize "me" time to regroup mentally so you can be the best YOU for your business and family.

PART III

UNDER THE HOOD

In any business, there are many specifics and things that you need to pay attention to that can give you a leg up on the competition. Racecar drivers know how important this is, but your average driver often doesn't check to see what's wrong until the "Check Engine" light goes on. We tend to be reactive instead of proactive. It's important to turn that around and do the things that will put you in a better position to reach those dreams we talked about earlier.

In business, you need to do the specific tasks that can make you stand out. In this section, we zero in on such tasks that will help you invent or reinvent yourself, brand yourself and your business, build your team, and preserve your hard-earned wealth. And finally, we talk about an important activity that's outside of the business realm: giving back.

8

inventing and reinventing yourself

When you are starting out you need to find what you are good at and push hard to "invent" yourself, so to speak. You need to really want it badly. You need to be hungry. Professional athletes make it to the highest levels by pushing themselves. They stay longer than other players at the gym and work harder on their skills. Michael Jordan and Kobe Bryant would practice an hour or more shooting even before the official practice began. Other top athletes have had similar personal routines that have set them apart from their peers. It's also about having the drive to stick with it no matter what. Consider how long it took Harrison Ford to make his dream of becoming an actor come true. He was 36 years old when he was finally able to quit his carpenter job and earn a living acting in movies like *Star Wars*. Plenty of business owners got started and hit their stride later in life as well, such as Colonel Harland David Sanders who was 56 when he founded Kentucky Fried Chicken after many failed businesses. Then there's Richard Branson who founded

Virgin Cola, Virgin Vodka, Virgin Cosmetics, Virginware (lingerie) and Virgin Cars, among many other failed businesses before he saw great success with Virgin America. These and many other athletes, actors, business owners, and ordinary individuals like myself, have one thing in common . . . drive.

I was driven to find success any way I could—every time I met somebody, I'd listen to what they had to say and what they did for a living and, in many cases, if I thought it was a good idea, I'd latch onto the idea and say, "I'll try it." I did this with about a dozen businesses before I landed in real estate.

Stay Determined and Find Your Passion

I admit, I had times when I was not very motivated, but I had a sense of resilience and I always bounced back quickly. My dream was to reach financial freedom without doing anything illegal. Throughout the years, I found new ventures and went into them knowing it might not work out. The key was finding the path to that critical mass. But, since nobody had a crystal ball, there was no way for sure of knowing which idea would be the one that worked for me. I didn't know I'd end up in real estate. Finding your path is important—finding your passion is also important. Then staying driven until you get to where you want to be is essential.

Rather than having a single, solitary focus, it helps to open yourself up to various opportunities so you will have a better chance of finding something that works for you. But you need to be searching with an open mind and looking at everything as an opportunity. You have to keep an open mind and keep inventing yourself.

Too many people are not open to new opportunities. In other cases, they are determined to do what they want on their own terms. But, if there is no market for it, or they focus on themselves rather than on the customers, they end up with a failed business. In other cases, people find an opportunity they really like but walk away too soon without giving it enough time. Often, they fail to put in the hours and research to find the best path to making it work. If I lost my drive and walked away from real estate after my first failed deal, I would not be

My Car Business

At one time when I was in my 20s, I started my own business selling cars. I'd pick up *Auto Trader* magazine every Wednesday as soon as it came out, which was very early in the morning, and I'd sit and read it in my car with a flashlight looking for good deals until the sun came up. Then I'd try to be the first one there to buy the car. I was looking for cars priced below market that I could buy, fix up, and sell for more money. Remember—buying something, improving upon it, and reselling it is a way for making nice profits. This is the basic idea behind flipping houses, not to mention how many other businesses operate.

I learned a little about cars when I was a door-to-door mechanic's helper, as I mentioned earlier. I ran my car selling business for about two years. I'd buy a car for around $500 and after fixing it up, sell it for $800 or more. Honda Accords and BMWs were both very popular in Garden Grove, California, where I was living with my parents at the time. Honestly, I thought that this would be a huge moneymaker and eventually I would open my own lot. I liked the opportunity because people need cars and want them to look good and run well. Unfortunately, in the end it didn't work out, so I called it quits. But, rather than sulk, I just moved on to another opportunity and another one after that.

where I am today, and you would not be reading this book. I knew that I had found my passion and that no matter what, I had to stay driven.

When you stay driven for as long as I have, you eventually find the right path. It's all about persistence and a need to keep on building on that mindset.

Do You Really Want It?

It's important to gauge your desire when it comes to thinking about your goals, both personal and professional. You have to really want it . . . and if you want it badly enough you'll find a way and, somehow, you'll get there. The forces of the universe work in a crazy way and at some point, you end up crossing paths with the right people. That, along with the powers of your subconscious and, yes, a little bit of luck, can sometimes make the stars align for you.

You can, however, make it easier on yourself by engaging with people around you. Remember, I struck up a conversation with the landlord from my supermarket when I was sitting in a court room. He opened my eyes to real estate. If I had had my head down or was staring at my cell phone like so many people are doing today, I might never have had that conversation and might not have made a serious effort to get into real estate. Face-to-face connections are the catalysts for the business world—take advantage of them whenever you can.

To really want something badly, you need to have a source of motivation. What is motivating you to succeed and to stay on the path to your destination? Where is your drive coming from? For many people, it's a desire to provide your family with a good life or have the financial freedom to buy the finer things in life. Desperation and escaping poverty are also strong motivating factors; they certainly were for me. I was desperate to get far away from the hardship that I experienced when my family came here. I never wanted to go back to living in a car and was going to keep on trying to do better no matter what life threw at me.

I also felt a lot of pressure to help my family get through the financial hardship we were experiencing. I was laser focused on becoming successful and making the pain of loss and struggle go away. Had I been born into a lot of money, I probably wouldn't have tried so hard. To be honest with you, sometimes it's better to be poor or come from "humble beginnings." It gives you tremendous motivation to be successful. Having a lot of money can make you too comfortable. This isn't to say that many people who come from money don't work hard to succeed on their own and go on to do great things. However, for others, the comfort holds them back.

When you really want something, it becomes a part of who you are. People knew me as someone who was always determined and ready to take a new approach to get to where I wanted to be. My friends always knew that I was the ambitious one, and even now when I run into some old friends, they tell me, "I always knew you would get here." People can tell when you are driven.

Stay on Track

Once you find your source of motivation, cultivate your passion, and "invent" yourself, staying on track is important. To do that, I set up weekly and yearly goals. I find that yearly goals are supercritical for me. They are goals I want to reach at some point during the year, sometimes personal goals as well as business goals. I know, however, that they will take a while, so I do not anticipate reaching yearly goals quickly. I review my yearly goals every month to see how much progress I've made. If I'm not making progress, I pick up the pace.

A World of Distractions

It's very easy to go off track with so many distractions around us. Many people spend hours talking with friends and family on Facebook or posting on other social media platforms. Then they look at the clock and realize how little they've accomplished in the course of the day.

Thanks to technology, we have so many more ways to distract ourselves from our goals. It gets harder and harder to stay the course. But, if you are going to succeed, you need to have the willpower to turn the television off, stop texting your friends, turn off the video games, or get off social media and force yourself to get away from the distractions. It's too easy to occupy your time with reality TV and get away from going after your goals. Set time limits and stick to them—even shorter lunch breaks can keep you working toward your goals.

You can then reward yourself at the end of the week when you've completed all of the items you had planned for that week. Treat yourself and your family to a great dinner or go to a show—you've earned it by giving 100 percent and completing your weekly list of things you planned to accomplish. Growing up, I never played sports or hung out with friends on weekends. Instead, I worked seven days a week. That was the sacrifice I made so that I could get here quicker. I always tell people to work super hard and to save and invest for a few years so that you can enjoy a high-quality life in the future. Life is often about sacrificing a little now to see bigger and better things later.

▲ chapter 8 / inventing and reinventing yourself

As for the weekly goals, I make a list of what I need to accomplish and check the items off line by line as I go through the week. These lists are critical for me to stay on the right track. If you don't write goals down, you can get lazy, go on vacations, and do other things that are unproductive. Pretty soon, you'll see that six months have gone by, and you're nowhere closer to your goal than when you started the year.

Whether you keep a daily "to do" list or work from a weekly list, you want to look at it often and prioritize what you need to do next, then check each item off or delete it from your phone as you go. This is super important when it comes to being productive: when you write things down, your mind is also taking mental notes and your subconscious is working in the background for you. I have been writing down my daily, weekly, and yearly goals since I was 16! If you're looking for an app to help manage your schedule and keep track of goals, you might check out Todoist, OmniFocus, or even Planner Pro.

Reinventing Yourself

Reinventing yourself means you have to accept and agree to change yourself, which may mean the way you think, the way you live, the people you associate with, the way you do business, and so forth. I started working at the early age of 14, and from that point on, I changed who I was and what I was doing many times over. I had the same goal of becoming successful and having financial freedom, but I reinvented myself many times along the way. I'm not the same person I was at 14, 20, 25, or 35. As you grow and mature, your priorities change and you gain valuable resources to help you achieve your goals. This is partly because of your life situation, being single or married or having children, but also because you keep powering up—learning more, networking with new people, and exposing yourself to new ideas.

The world around you keeps changing, so you need to adapt and explore. If you don't stay current, you run the risk of falling behind and missing opportunities. It is often the case that when businesses don't make changes and reinvent themselves, they will fall behind their competition. If, for example, I was not staying on top of the latest real estate deals on the internet and was instead using more antiquated technology, I might have missed out on many profitable opportunities. This happens in businesses all the time. When a business becomes comfortable doing things a certain way, they fail to keep up with their competitors. In other businesses, it's not about "having" to reinvent themselves but a desire to expand into something new.

Either way, whether you need to reinvent yourself to stay current or want to add a new "flavor" to your business, you have to keep on learning. For example, here I am, almost 50, and I'm still learning new things. In recent years, I've been learning a lot about technology. I've been buying and selling real estate for years, but now I started to invest in other startup tech businesses. I even started my own venture: I launched an app called Fuzul that is doing very well. Apps are not something that even existed 20 or 30 years ago, so if I had not reinvented myself with a focus on technology, Fuzul would not have happened.

Some people reinvent themselves and take an entirely new path. Consider LEGO®, the toy company. Many years ago, they sold wooden blocks, but after a fire burned the business down, they decided to reinvent themselves with the famous interlocking plastic toys. More recently, they expanded—while not ridding themselves of their "Holy Grail" (the toys)—by going into the film business with LEGO® *Batman* and other movies.

So, you may wonder how I, a long-time commercial real estate investor, reinvented myself and expanded into the technical world. As with everything in my life, it was a journey down an as-yet unexplored path.

Expanding Limits

I have been reading and following several rankings of business people for years going back to the late 1990s, and I noticed that there were more billionaires in the technology sector progressing upward on these lists than there were in any other industry. Yes, there are a lot of industries represented, including real estate, retail merchandising, and the oil and gas industry, among others that are related to tycoons, but the top tier of the list, since I've been reading it, has always featured technology. I also knew that technology was one sector that is going to dominate for years to come. So, with that information, I wanted to come up with a company that would use technology to help people run their business and their lives more efficiently.

One day, I was having a parking lot repaved at one of my large shopping centers in Pennsylvania, and a vendor wanted payment. I realized how cool it would be if I could post a job on an app to have a local resident in the area go out and do a live streaming video or take lots of photos of the job for me so I could see how the job was going before rendering payment. Being in California, it's hard to see what's going on with properties hundreds or thousands of miles away. I do have property managers but, in this case, he was only able to visit the shopping center once a week. I thought, "what if someone could be my eyes in the many different places I was having work done on my properties?"

It was from that experience that the light bulb went on in my head and the idea for Fuzul, which in Farsi means "nosy person," was born. Two years and a few hundred thousand dollars later, and I am suddenly in the tech business—who knew that would happen? Now here I am with my app in the app store. It's new territory for me, my first rodeo you might say, and I'm excited about it.

Fuzul is an app that utilizes a smartphone's camera to give you the opportunity to be in as many as 10 or 20 places at once. It is an on-demand marketplace of eyes-for-hire.

My first test for Fuzul came when Leyla and I were discussing that she has products from her business in numerous stores and locations, but she can't fly or drive to all the stores to check up on inventory and to see if everything is displayed properly. So, we decided to test out the new app. We posted jobs offering $10 each for people to go into each of the stores and let us see through their smartphone's cameras if the racks were in the correct places and to make sure the products were properly displayed. Within two hours we had videos coming in. It was awesome! She was able to call the stores and place orders with them on the items they were out of, which more than paid for the Fuzul jobs!

The whole dynamic of the job market has changed; people are thinking in terms of a Google mentality, an Apple mentality, a Facebook mentality, or a YouTube or Instagram mentality. In other words, the social media platforms that people gravitate toward and use regularly inform their worldview greatly. So, when you think about how to integrate your business into the social/technology world, consider your business' key demographics and cater to the social approach that works for your product or service and audience. This taps into the immediacy of how tasks can be reviewed through a simple technological application connecting people in the area of the jobs and utilizing your time efficiently!

For the people responding to the job postings on Fuzul, it's kind of like Uber, a way to make a few bucks on your own terms and through your own vehicle—although with Fuzul, it's not your car but your smartphone. For someone like me, with properties in several states, I can post a job in the specific area of a property and hire somebody to be my eyes (or do a task) in another state. They can show me in real time how construction is going, if the trees have been trimmed, or if they have put in the new concrete. It's the only simple app that allows you to monetize the camera on your phone using GPS and location services. For example, when you sign up, it will send you push notifications of all new jobs within a three-mile radius. If you go on vacation, you can still do a few jobs in the area and make a few bucks while on vacation. Fuzul first launched in early 2017 in the Apple App Store and in early 2018 on the Google Play Store and has gained more and more traction. You can learn more by visiting www.fuzul.com.

What's Your Fuzul?

Do you have the drive to reinvent yourself? Can you start fresh or add something to your repertoire?

The way to reinvent yourself is to stay on top of what is trending in the world, what is popular, and what people are excited about. Right now, people are using their smartphones more than their computers or their tablets, so we found a way to tap into that reality with a mobile app that served both my business and Leyla's business, as well as to help business owners who have expanded out of their local or regional areas.

People are using technology to change their businesses and revolutionize industries. For example, a couple of successful theatrical producers recently created the first online platform that streams Broadway shows digitally so that people in other parts of the world can see what it's like to be in a seat at a Broadway show. They reinvented themselves with a new streaming technology business. Some major companies have completely reinvented themselves over the years as well, such as American Express. It went from being an express mail carrier to a credit card giant. More recently, American Express ventured into new technology partnering with Google and Apple on mobile wallets. Netflix used to send DVDs by mail to its customers, and now it's a huge online network featuring movies and original programming. And let's remember that Amazon started out only as an online bookseller. Celebrities recreate themselves as well, such as one of my favorites when I first came to America, Arnold Schwarzenegger, who went from professional bodybuilder to a successful acting career to governor of California and back to acting. And how about George Foreman? He was a heavyweight champion. Now he is world famous for the hugely popular George Foreman Grills.

The point is, you don't have to keep on doing what you have always been doing if you are falling behind or simply want to expand your repertoire—the world keeps changing, and you can reinvent yourself to change with it. The problem is that many people have a good, or even fantastic, idea and they tell other people all about it, but it stops right there. They don't actually *do* anything about it. They don't have the drive to keep on going in a new direction. Perhaps, they're scared.

You need to have a passion and a sense of adventure, to start exploring and start powering up once again to see if it is a feasible idea. If it makes sense and you have a new destination, then you need to start planning how you will get there. Of course, I have the means to do something with an idea, but if I didn't have the money, I would have kept pitching the idea again and again to people who have the money until I got someone willing to invest. That's what the TV programs *Shark Tank* and *Entrepreneur Elevator Pitch* are all about. People are trying to reinvent themselves with a great idea for a new product or service.

Getting Too Complacent

Many people find that once they reach some level of success with a pizza shop, repair service, mortgage company, or any type of business, they often become too comfortable. They don't try as hard anymore, but then they want a bigger house or a nicer car. The only way to get those things is to expand and grow the business, take on new challenges, network, and be on the lookout for the next opportunity. It doesn't mean that you quit your job or sell your business. It means that you explore other options and try to find a way in which to add to what you do or reinvent yourself.

There's no real magic to reinventing yourself. I'm still always looking to upgrade by trying new ideas that make sense to me. I'm always doing research online, looking to educate myself, and seeking successful people that I can learn from. I believe it's important to stay active and productive. Part of that includes exercise, eating right, and

Attitude Counts!

Reinventing yourself is also about having the right attitude. Remember, attitude is everything. You have to get up with a positive attitude and when negative things happen, you have to try a different tactic. Staying positive is super important. I always tell everybody to start your day with a big smile and a nice cup of coffee or tea. If you are a bitter person, who is always complaining, no one will want to hang out with you. If you have a positive attitude, people will want to talk to you and then who knows what you can learn from them.

▲ chapter 8 / inventing and reinventing yourself

taking care of yourself. How can you reinvent yourself if the "new you" is too worn out and out of shape to take on the new opportunities that arise?

Remember, you won't end up being rich if you don't try, so you'll simply have to keep on trying.

 YOUR ROADMAP TO SUCCESS

► When you are first inventing yourself or finding your passion, you need to be driven and have a burning desire to succeed.

► Be open to many possibilities.

► Reinventing yourself can mean making a complete makeover or expanding what you do into a significant new area of interest.

► You need to have the same enthusiasm for the new venture as you have for your current business.

► Reinventing yourself doesn't mean taking on a hobby; it means taking your career in a new direction or an additional direction.

► Don't let yourself get caught up with distractions.

► Keep powering up—look for good ideas and a market that is not oversaturated.

9

preserving
wealth

Making money is only half the battle—keeping it is the other half. Yet if you read financial publications, far more than 50 percent of the articles are about ways to make money. Saving money doesn't make for great headlines, but it's vital to your long-term success.

Unfortunately, the compulsion to buy everything in sight can overwhelm people and spending becomes like an addiction. Then there are those who get swallowed up by the vultures who surround them. Wealth attracts many people who want a piece of what you've earned. They want to somehow be on your payroll, and if you don't watch out, you can have far too many people in your entourage taking your hard-earned money.

Consider how many celebrities have made a fortune and then given it all away through frivolous spending and paying too many people to do everything for them. Quite a few famous names have had to file for bankruptcy. Therefore, regardless of how you make money, you need plans for how to preserve it. Remember, it's not how much you make; it's how much you get to keep. With that in mind, I want to discuss a few important ways that can help preserve your wealth.

(Full disclosure: I am not an attorney, and this is not meant as professional legal advice. Such advice should come from a practicing attorney. I am sharing tips that have worked for me and what I've learned over the years. Your mileage may vary.)

Create an Estate Plan and Establish a Trust

Find a reputable attorney who specializes in estate planning. There are many reasons to establish a family trust, some of which are: asset protection, a plan and guide to continue your legacy after your death, to provide for your family, tax benefits, supporting your favorite cause, avoiding probate court (which is a lengthy process for your family to go through to get your assets), and many more. I established my trust in 2002 and have amended it many times, as my life has progressed and changed over the years with kids, new properties, philanthropic causes, and my future plans. **This is a must**.

Set up an SPE (Single Purpose Entity) for Each Investment

Are you protected against liability? In a very litigious society, it is quite easy for somebody to maliciously file a lawsuit against you. Suppose someone takes a bad fall on your property, and they sue you for $5 million. It doesn't even have to be something that obvious—someone can sue you because they invested with you and didn't make money. So, what can you do? How you hold ownership in each asset is crucial; you don't want all your assets (particularly properties) to be under your trust. I set up my businesses and properties as separate entities from my trust. I take that one step further by having all the properties and businesses I own in their own separate SPE (single purpose entity). This means that the members of that LLC are in my trust, so it gives me another layer of protection. You should work with your estate planner and CPA to determine what suits you the best. There have been business owners who were sued for the slightest nuances in a contract. Make sure your money is protected.

Consider a Good Financial Advisor

As for investing, if you seek a financial advisor, make sure to find one who takes your needs into consideration based on your financial goals and risk tolerance. You also want someone who will help diversify your investments accordingly. Many financial advisors try to sell you investment products that may not be the best ones suited for you, so do your own research before you commit. No one will care more about your money than you!

I have been investing my own money ever since I came to America. Sure, I have made bad decisions and taken some missteps, but the lessons I learned have been invaluable. I toyed with the stock market several times and still invest in the market today, but I believe that real estate is the best investment. For this reason, I do not invest a significant percent of my assets in stocks, bonds, and annuities. I do, however, recommend having some form of investments that give you liquidity and diversification. If you have the time and patience to do research on a regular basis, there are many ways to easily invest on your own. For those of you who have little time to do research and study the best options, a reputable financial advisor may be the way to go.

Unfortunately, I've heard many horror stories where investors are sold an investment vehicle, or an endowment fund, and then when the market goes down and they want to pull their money out, they are hit with penalties in addition to losing principle. Often, this is because the instruments that were sold had the highest commissions, which is why the advisor selected them.

Therefore, even if you find a financial advisor, do your research before agreeing to any investment or working with any advisor. You can't totally trust anyone else with your hard-earned money. One of the reasons why the people mentioned earlier went bankrupt is because they got bad advice. Remember, nobody will care as much about protecting your money than you. There are tons of websites that you can go to and read about stocks and mutual funds to help you determine which ones meet your needs and your level of risk tolerance. So, roll up your sleeves and do your online research.

Diversify

A good financial advisor will make sure you are well diversified; you will want to diversify so you don't have all your eggs in one basket. So, if you have $500,000 to invest, you want to possibly have 20 percent invested in the stock market, again making sure that 20 percent is diversified into several different products which could be: fixed income, emerging markets, tech stocks, bonds, etc. Then, have 20 percent in cash. It's critical you have liquidity so that as opportunities present themselves you'll be able to tap into your cash to take advantage of them—this is your working capital. Lastly, I would have 60 percent in real estate. Here, too, you can diversify in the different classes of real estate. You can diversify into industrial, office, retail strip malls, and apartments buildings. Each of these asset classes bear different risks. For example, buying a retail strip center with four or five national tenants is much less risky than an office building with a single non-credit tenant; although the single non-credit tenant may have a much higher cash flow, it does bear a lot more risk. I have spread my investments around in several categories. For example, I have some retail centers that give me stabilized cash flow and some office buildings that are more of a value-add play, so I lease them up and flip them. I also have some out-of-state retail offices that have a higher cash flow and are occupied by non-credit tenants.

Diversification helps you spread your money around over more and less risky ventures. For me, it means investing in real estate and in cars. For someone else, it might mean the stock market and precious metals, or perhaps it means commodities and valuable art works. The point is, while the economy does see strong ties between markets, you can diversify into areas that are less interrelated.

Find a Good CPA and Listen to Them

It's important that you remember it's not how much you make but how much you get to keep. Tax laws keep changing and you need to have someone who is on top of the latest changes working on your behalf and providing you with sound tax advice. That being said, it doesn't mean that you do not need to know anything about taxes and how they affect your investments or benefits. Even with a CPA, you should familiarize yourself with some of the tax basics.

One of the things I like most about real estate is that along with making a great profit, there are tax advantages. Unlike the stock market or selling a car, which will produce realized gains (and you will have to pay Uncle Sam), real estate is one of the only investment vehicles that will allow you to defer the gains so that you will not have a large tax bill when you sell. This is why many wealthy individuals are in real estate, because you have all the flexibility and tax benefits.

The other huge benefit of real estate is depreciation. This refers to the gradual loss of value of a building due to normal wear and tear over its life. For commercial properties, they spread it over 39 years so if you buy a building for $2,000,000 and it's assessed $1,500,000 for improvements and $500,000 for land, then the $1,500,000 value is spread over 39 years thereby giving you $38,461 per year in depreciation expense! Itemizing depreciation as an expense will reduce your taxable income. You can even take that one step further and accelerate the depreciation by doing a cost segregation study (this is where all property-related costs that can be depreciated over 5, 7, and 15 years are identified). As a result, you will have an increased cash flow, which allows you the liquidity to act quickly when the right deal comes along and to let you preserve your wealth in real estate.

While not all investments have the tax benefits of real estate, a good tax adviser will find legal ways to minimize your tax bill to fit your specific situation. Just make sure whomever you are working with is credible and has a good reputation. Bad tax advice or trying to hide money from the government in offshore accounts is not advisable. The IRS has a way of catching onto people. Remember, Al Capone was not caught and sent to jail by the FBI, CIA, or the police. It was Uncle Sam and the IRS. So, whatever you do to minimize your tax bill, make sure it's on the up and up.

However, it's not all up to your tax advisor. If you want to benefit from an expert's help, make sure to keep good records not just around tax time, but all year long. Document everything that involves income and make everything accessible to your tax specialist.

Seek Good Legal Advice

Good legal advice is essential in preserving your wealth. Face it, when you make it to the top, you can become a target. As mentioned above, you need to protect your assets against predators. Sometimes just bad advice on structuring a deal can be very costly for you.

Back in 2007, I was buying a building with nine or ten other investors, and I was advised to set it up as a TIC (tenant in common), which meant that we would all share a specified proportion of ownership rights in the property, so we all took title to the property as TICs each with our share of ownership. We later lost the single tenant and were forced to sell the property with a large loss, and one of the partners took legal action against my company. If I had better legal advice at the time, I would have avoided painful litigation. Thankfully, my current attorney has been great and has helped me avoid many pitfalls.

Lawyers should also review all business contracts, even those among family and friends with whom you are doing business. And if there is a dispute, ask the lawyer for some advice before saying, or doing, something you may regret. Real estate lawyers are typically well versed in the nuances that go into a lease.

In most businesses, you can find someone with specific knowledge of your field. Having someone who has experience with the problems you may face can help you protect yourself—he or she can read the fine print and steer you away from making bad decisions.

As you can imagine, I get approached with many business opportunities and the ones that pique my interest I share with my attorney. A few years ago, I was approached with a business opportunity that involved a big brand of speakers that were being sold in many large retail stores, such as Best Buy. It was a million dollar investment that would give me partnership interest in an international company. My attorney, Matt, advised me to run from the opportunity as he saw many red flags that I hadn't noticed mainly regarding the ownership and their trademark. After doing some research, he found out the partner had already sold the trademark and had many past, and pending, legal issues. I took his advice, but the friend of mine, who had presented this deal to me, went ahead and invested. He ended up losing over a million dollars and is still in litigation with the company today.

Stick to What Has Been Working for You—Don't Go Chasing the Next Hot Investment

Commercial real estate and investing in automobiles are two areas that I am most comfortable with when it comes to investing. I stay with them because they have worked very well for me, and because cars are also a hobby of mine. I have occasionally ventured away from real estate, but I always return. There's an old saying—don't fix what isn't broken, and real estate is not broken for me.

Nonetheless, when I was asked by a friend to go in on a bitcoin investment, I made a relatively small investment. I did it mostly to be supportive, knowing that this was not an area I was well versed in, and had some doubts about cryptocurrencies in general. I prefer investing in something tangible, like buildings and cars, which you can see and touch.

You also need to be careful when the next big trend comes along and is sweeping up people like a tornado. You don't want to let yourself get swept up in the excitement unless you can get in and out quickly without taking too great a risk. At the turn of the last century, in the late 1990s, people were jumping into the dotcoms at an amazing rate. The dotcom craze however, only lasted until the dotcom crash. Sure, if you were an early investor in Google or Yahoo!, you did great, but what about the many people putting good money behind one of the many, many dotcoms that went belly up? In the end, a lot of people lost a lot of money. Others, who worked for the dotcoms walked away with worthless stock options.

The problem with the latest money making trends is that they do not have a track record. There is no success to look back on. Plus, the newest trends tend to draw too many people all looking to cash in on the same opportunities. The thousands of new dotcoms eventually boiled down to the few biggies that make a fortune today, like Amazon, Facebook, and Google. The same thing happened when the automobile first came out nearly a century earlier. There were roughly 80 early carmakers in the United States. In a short time, only a few—Ford, Chevrolet, GM, and some others—remained.

There's nothing wrong with dabbling in something new, but look for something that is not so oversaturated that it's impossible for everyone to profit. Even in the gold rush of 1848, when 300,000 people descended on California to find their fortune, many came back with nothing to show for their efforts.

Also, remember to make sure that whatever cash you are investing consists of extra funds that you can afford to lose. It's like hitting a casino once in a while. You do so with the understanding that this is not your primary means of making money, but a side-venture and you gamble only money that you can afford to lose. Too many people don't do this and fall into tremendous debt.

When it comes to significant funding, you should not venture too far out of your wheelhouse whether you are investing or even expanding your business. For example, many businesses have tried to expand outside of their fields, but few have succeeded. This also crosses over into reinventing themselves, as discussed earlier. For example, when a successful airline parts maker decided that they would build equipment for other modes of transportation, they learned quickly that the light equipment necessary for an airplane to fly did not meet the needs of buses and trains—it was a whole different ballgame. On a smaller level, the company behind the 100-year-old candy Life Savers once decided to go into the soda business—so they made Life Savers soda with the same bright colors. It didn't last long. There was also the time that Colgate, the toothpaste maker, decided to try making dinner entrees, which did not catch on—who wants to buy frozen dinners from a toothpaste

P.F. Chang's Meets Benihana . . . or Not

I must admit that even after going into real estate and enjoying success, I have also been seduced by other investment options and my own dreams. I always wanted to open a sushi restaurant, build it into a great place to eat, and then open ten or twelve more restaurants around the country. So, I bought a restaurant for $2.2 million in 2007. It was a free-standing building on 40-year-leased land, which at the time, was a steakhouse. I wanted to transform it into a P.F. Chang's meets Benihana. I was excited about it because people were making good money in 2007 and spending much of that money on drinks and food. The problem, however, was that the location wasn't in a city that had good wage earners and could frequent restaurants often. I also had no restaurant experience.

Although I had run a number of businesses over the years, there is nothing quite as challenging as a restaurant. With a restaurant, you have to perform perfectly every day. Some, with multiple locations, make money because the good locations are like the rock stars and carry the others. To make it work, first you need great service. Plus, you also need to have terrific food and ambiance. Then you need to be consistent. Without these key things, people will not come back. Also, like fashion, you have to constantly refresh your menu every year or every six months to keep up with tastes and trends. For example, restaurants today are offering healthier options and gluten-free menu items. And of course, everything has to be fresh. On top of all that, the margins are also really small, so you need to know how much to order so you do not end up wasting a lot of food.

You also need a good location. I remember interviewing several general managers and they told me this location would never make money—so that was an eye-opener. I had to swallow my ego. The worst part was perhaps that I was so excited about owning a restaurant that I, a real estate person, forgot the old adage: location, location, location. But, there were two things that I did that you should always do:

1. I invested money on an unfamiliar venture that I could afford to lose.

2. I got out fast. When something is crumbling or you realize you made a mistake and you see no easy way to turn it around and make it work, find the nearest exit.

P.F. Chang's Meets Benihana . . . or Not, continued

There is no positive result to putting in good money after bad. If you stand to lose a reasonable amount, don't let that loss become a major fortune by not getting out. Remember, you have to know when to fold. So, I leased it, and while it only gives me very small cash flow it was better than losing thousands of dollars running my own restaurant.

company? The point is, don't stray too far from what you do well unless you have a lot of money and the risk tolerance to make some risky investments. I still feel the disappointment of my attempt at opening a sushi restaurant.

This isn't to say that with some expert advice and doing a lot of research, you can't start something new—I did so with the app I developed—but we put in two years and had experts leading the way. Therefore, if you are going to branch out and invest or start a business outside of your comfort zone, do your research, learn a lot, call in an expert and be ready to get out before you take a major loss.

Consider Collectibles

One area that I recommend for investors is collectibles. Typically, collectibles and rare artistic and historical items are a good place to stash money because they continue to increase in value. While most people will not have a valuable work of art, like the Leonardo da Vinci painting that recently sold for $430 million, there is value in collectibles. This can range from antique furniture to rare coins to rare cars, baseball cards, journals, posters, and so forth. Maintained in good condition, collectibles have a long-term value. Again, you must study the market in which you collect.

I still advocate staying primarily with what you know about and where you've had great success, whether that's real estate, fashion, technology, collectibles, or something else—whatever works for you.

Get Insured

This is probably one of the most important tips of all. Many people are under-insured, or not insured at all for certain catastrophes such as hurricanes, high winds, hail, flooding, etc. I learned about insurance the hard way. In 2008 I owned a large, nearly 800,000-square-foot industrial park on 40 acres of land in Houston. I had a blanket policy of $100 million for property with a $25,000 deductible per occurrence, but what I didn't know was that in the case of wind and hail (hurricane) my deductible would be 2 percent of the policy, so $2,000,000 instead of $25,000. After significant damage to my buildings from Hurricane Ike, I thought I was covered, and I was, but with a huge deductible. My damages were in the hundreds of thousands of dollars, but since it was less than the deductible, I ended up paying for it all out of pocket. That was a very expensive lesson! Make sure you have an experienced insurance broker who can tailor a policy that best suits you and your investments. As for liability insurance, some of the must-haves are covered in umbrella policies (these cover events over and beyond your regular liability policy limit) and E&O (errors and omissions). Depending on your business, there are many areas of coverage that would apply depending on your business and investments, so make sure you seek a reputable insurance broker.

Invest in Real Estate

Real estate has always been the basis of enormous wealth. If you want to have a financially free life, get your real estate license, educate yourself, and become a real estate agent/investor—even if you're not going to do sales or transactions, but just to understand what it means to invest in real estate.

No matter how you make money, real estate is the best way to preserve it because, for one thing, it is inflation proof. The costs of construction and labor are always going up historically—it costs much more to build now than it did five, six, or seven years ago. So, if you buy something that will cost much more 40 years from now, you are ahead of the game. You can then put the property or properties in a family trust, and you can always pass it on to your children.

Yes, there will be cycles in real estate, as there are in any market, but you will need to sit tight during the downturns like the recession of 2008, which lasted only a few years. In the long-term scheme of things, that's a short time period.

Earlier, I discussed some of the tax advantages of real estate. There are several and your CPA will help you take full advantage of them.

What I also like about real estate is that your investment doesn't have to sit dormant. While a stock or mutual fund will simply move up or down, unless you have a small dividend coming due regularly, your stock market investment can only show you a profit when you sell it. Until then, your profits are a paper gain and not yet a realized gain. Real estate, however, can make money for you while you own it by leasing it out. Right now, I have roughly 300 business tenants in my properties. This means that I do not have to sell an asset, such as an office building or shopping center, to make money. I lease out the space and collect rent.

Most of the focus of my first book was teaching the ordinary person the basics of real estate investing. I discussed the different classes of real estate: residential, commercial, retail, industrial, and so forth. There's a product for everybody. Some people, who love to roll up their sleeves and get busy, would be perfect as apartment owners. Others don't have time to deal with tenants, so they might own retail centers, which may have a tenant like Starbucks, for example. You don't need to babysit a Starbucks. They are corporate tenants and part of a larger company that will simply wire you your money. Otherwise, they take care of the food and oversee everything—so it's a hassle-free tenant.

Real estate really provides all kind of flexibility depending on your lifestyle, your personality, and how much you really want to get involved managing it. Plus, if you need money, you can refinance and get tax-free cash to do whatever you like.

Preserving your money is all about keeping it safe. This can sometimes mean minimizing your tax bills, taking precautions against those who want a piece of your money through litigation, maintaining your principle, and even profiting along the way, if possible. The goal of money preservation is to have something on which to retire and also to be able to pass something on to your children and even your grandchildren.

YOUR ROADMAP TO SUCCESS

▶ Form a family trust for asset protection and to help plan for your family after your death.

▶ Protect yourself against liability—a Single Purpose Entity (SPE) is a good idea.

▶ A financial advisor is not a must but can help you. Look for someone who understands your needs and is not simply selling off-the-rack products to make a commission.

▶ Diversify your investments to spread out your risk.

▶ Get a good CPA. Taxes are getting more and more difficult to understand, so make sure you have a professional who you trust advising you.

▶ Remember, it's not how much you make but how much you keep.

▶ Good legal advice is essential to preserving your wealth.

▶ Stick to what has been working for you. If you have knowledge and success in a specific area, stick with it.

▶ Chasing trends, fads, or the next hot investment idea can be dangerous.

▶ Don't skimp on insurance—explore all risks and get covered.

▶ Invest in real estate!

building your brand and building your team

Today, businesses market themselves all over social media, so as you start your business you'll also need to start focusing on branding early on in your career. Who you are and how people know you (or your business) can be just as important as what you do, if not more so.

If you look at almost anything that goes on around the world, nearly everything is in some way related to sales, even if it's not for monetary gain. For example, when you invite someone to your home for dinner, you are selling your hospitality. You want them to accept the invitation. When you go out to a club to meet someone, you are dressing up and making an effort to be personable to sell them on your personality and your appearance. When you go on an interview for a job, you are selling the interviewer on your skills, abilities, and who you are as a person. The way you present yourself, from your manner, personality, and opinions to your hair, clothes, and even your posture, says something about you. When you post on social media, for example, you are also presenting something about yourself. All of this packaged together is how you brand yourself as an individual.

If you want to be successful, branding is an essential component along with honing your skills and abilities. It all begins with the persona you present to your friends and family—it's who you are and what characterizes your personality. I started building a brand by always seeking out new opportunities. My friends knew that I was the guy always looking for the next opportunity, always dreaming of success, and always thinking of ways to get there. They knew I was ambitious.

Once you have a brand—something that defines you—it's time to start marketing yourself. I started marketing my personal brand on social media somewhat by accident. I enjoyed posting photos of my cars for other car lovers to see. I got a lot of responses. But pretty soon I realized that not only did people love the cars, they also wanted to know how I reached a point where I could own so many supercars. Eventually, every other comment was about how I made my money. That's what followers kept asking me: "How did you make so much money?"

I told them I'm in commercial real estate, and people started asking me if I could teach them how to get into real estate and make money at it. So, I realized that maybe I needed to write a book about how to make it in real estate—this became the premise of my first book. Then people wanted to know more about me and how can I help others develop the drive and ambition to succeed in real estate or in any other chosen profession, which brought me to this book. My books, along with my social media posts and the occasional television appearance or magazine interview, allow me to present my brand. In the coming sections, I'll share the things that helped me build and grow my brand.

Engaging with People

At both ends of any sale are human beings. Yes, you can buy a soda from a vending machine, but someone had to put the soda in the machine, and more significantly, someone had to make you aware of a specific brand and why you want to buy it. We all know Coke and Pepsi. Both major companies are international brands that now make many more products besides the familiar sodas. But there are many other soda makers out there. You know these two sodas because Coke and Pepsi branded them over many years until they became household names.

Businesses large and small need to engage people if they want customers. Building a brand means connecting with people and finding ways to inspire them because people like to be inspired—they like brands that make them feel good. An upbeat, positive message in a TV commercial or an online commercial makes people feel good, so it makes them want to connect with your brand. Conversely, a charity may tug at your heartstrings so that you feel empathy and connect emotionally. It's psychological—if your brand doesn't make people respond emotionally then you're doing something wrong.

What's so important about building your personal brand is that it's how people come to define you. People will think of me as Manny, the successful real estate guy with the amazing car collection. Perhaps you're the personable, noted chef and restaurant owner who comes out and meets all the customers. Your brand is how people can define you and what's so important is that once you've built your brand, no one can take away your brand from you—that's the beauty of it. You can't worry that someone is going to invent it better; it's your name, and it's your persona. There's only one of you and that's priceless. Once you realize you are unique and start working on branding yourself, it can have a ripple effect as more and more people like what they see. While social media can speed up the process, branding yourself can take years. However, at some point you will realize you have grown a large following, and you can use that for networking, marketing, driving customers to your business, or simply as a thought leader, inspiring the world.

I have received hundreds of business inquiries through social media from my followers. While many have requested funding for their ideas/startups, a few have been real estate related, and some have been great for me. For example, one of my followers on Instagram, who is a mortgage broker for a very large lender in New York City, messaged me pitching real estate financing with very attractive rates. So, the next time I needed financing, I looked him up and asked myself, "What do I have to lose?" I decided to have him bid on a $16 million dollar loan that, at the time, I was trying to refinance. I put out bids to two local lenders and to him. As it turned out, he came in with the best terms. He was young, hungry, and fought for me to get a better loan, and he even took a lower fee. I was very happy and have continued to give him business. I have probably done over $80 million dollars in financing with him since that first deal. The point is, when you build a good brand, people want to do business with you. It opens up opportunities.

Brand your business in a similar manner—ads, slogans, and logos are all designed to convey a message that engages people. But they all need to convey the right message to your market. Businesses use everything from the right spokespeople to the right visuals and the right colors to the right sounds to brand themselves so they can present the right image. Then, they need to stay consistent across all forms of media.

All of this takes some time to create, but once you have the pieces together that best represent your business, you can stand out from the competition. There are so many brands that we know because they've made a conscious effort to engage us and make us feel good about their product(s) or services. We recognize the logos, the colors, the slogan, and so forth. If you're driving along and you see yellow arches over the trees, what restaurant are you approaching? What kind of food does it serve? If you have kids, will they want to go there? It's all branding.

Credibility

A successful person or business needs to be credible. There are many brands, businesses, and individuals that have lost their credibility and integrity over the years. Some manage to fool people for years.

Remember Enron and Bernie Madoff? You can present all sorts of messages about yourself or your business, but if you are not credible, people will see through it. If you are honest and people respect you, then credibility will be part of your brand, and people will want to do business with you. By being honest, never trying to con or scam anyone, I have built a reputation in real estate that has brokers coming to me with deals. They know I will be straight-forward, trustworthy, and act quickly. They know I am a closer!

It takes time, but gaining credibility comes from treating people fairly, listening, being consistent, gaining people's trust, and if you make a mistake, acknowledging it. Today, we hear about many businesses and individuals deceiving people, which will totally ruin their credibility. It can take a long time to gain it back. It's like your credit score. You need to build up the score by paying your credit card bills on time and staying out of debt, because once your credit rating goes south, it takes time to rebuild it.

Marketing Your Brand

First, determine what it is that people like about you or your company, and then use that to brand yourself. For me, it turned out to be my

Credibility Matters

If, for example, the Irvine Company (one of the largest landlords in the United States) needs a $1 million line of credit, they will most likely have no problem getting it quickly. However, if some landlord walks in with the same request and has not established any credibility in the marketplace—that landlord will have a much harder time getting a line of credit. Credibility also matters when something goes wrong—rather than deserting you, customers will give you much greater latitude if they know you are a credible company that made a mistake. Credibility is a form of trust and that goes a long way in business. Also, keep in mind that if you lose your credibility, it's hard to get it back.

collection of supercars that generated attention. So, I've built on that following, and then branched out into letting those followers get to know more about me, such as how I got here and what I do today.

Remember, people want to get inspired, so share your journey and what you are passionate about. If you're an artist, share your art. If you are a stock trader, share some tips and strategies. If you are a chef, share some recipes. If you are a car collector, share information about your cars. Let them know the back-story as you share your brand.

These are some ways you can reach people:

- *Start a YouTube channel.* YouTube is great for SEO (search engine optimization) since Google owns them and gives priority on their search rankings. Take some time to make your videos appealing and get your message across in an entertaining way. The most unusual videos go viral, so think about what you could do that will make people tell their friends about you. One video series of a mysterious woman (doesn't show her face) opening Disney toys and describing them, earned her nearly $5 million dollars—really. Even more amazing, a six-year old also raked in over a million dollars doing the same thing, opening toys. Of course, you need to monetize to make money online by building up your following and selling advertising or subscriptions.
- *Create short ebooks and offer them for free as lead generation* to promote what you do and to gain more potential customers. Others create longer books promoting themselves and their expertise. This leads to speaking engagements or interviews on television, webinars, or podcasts. This results in great brand awareness.
- *Post on social media sites regularly.* Instagram, Facebook, Twitter, and LinkedIn are the most well-known platforms, but there are others. Photos help you grow your brand on Instagram, while Facebook is about posting and sharing content and videos with your audience and fans, so businesses need to have a presence in front of the billion-plus users. LinkedIn focuses more on business, while Twitter is about sharing current events and talking with people who have common interests. Each site has their own unique angle in the marketplace. By

using some of the social media platforms often, you can grow a following. But your content has to be genuine and unique, and you have to know what will entice your followers to return. You don't have to post every day, but you should post several times a week to keep followers coming back while also getting new ones. Be consistent in your message and get to know what your followers like the most. Also, be careful that you don't get redundant, boring, or become that pushy annoying salesperson that people meet at parties and always want to get away from. Social media is about building connections and relationships, not hitting people over the head with a sales pitch. Remember, people can easily delete, stop following you, or unsubscribe.

▶ *Teach classes, do seminars, lead webinars, or host podcasts.* Remember to keep it interesting and have takeaways since people want to get something out of your talk. Many brands today also generate a lot of attention for the work they do helping others or benefitting the environment. Your brand is not only about what you sell but what you stand for.

▶ *Utilize promotional items.* Get your name out there in front of people. That's why businesses give out all sorts of promotional items like caps, T-shirts, mugs, pens, and all sorts of items with

King of the Hill

When it comes to branding, Ferrari is widely considered the world's most successful brand. In fact, almost 30 percent of Ferrari's profits actually come from branding, which includes licensing the name, badge, and logo as well as having a major retail line of jackets, headwear, eyewear, and many other products. While most people cannot afford to actually own a Ferrari, the company is marketing the excitement behind the cars, their rich racing history, the beauty of the cars, and their expert craftsmanship. They even have a museum at their factory. The point is, Ferrari is selling a dream and it's one that millions of people have including me.

▲ chapter 10 / building your brand and building your team

your name and logo on them. It keeps your brand in front of people, and it's cheaper than advertising.

▶ *Utilize product placement.* This means getting your product(s) on television, in movies, videos, and in other forms of media. How often are you watching a TV show or a movie where someone opens an Apple laptop? That's amazing product placement and so much less expensive than creating advertisements.

▶ *Sponsor an event.* This could be a community event, something for a local charity, a sporting event, etc. Brands become associated with sponsoring certain events.

Remember, you need to brand not only yourself and your business but the emotional connection people get from your product or service. If your product makes people feel good, make sure that's part of your branding strategy.

Also—very important—don't stop branding when you become successful. Many popular brands disappear over the years because they assume that everyone knows all about them. You not only need to keep branding yourself, but you need to find new connections between what you offer as an individual or a business and the next generation. Twenty years ago, I could not reach out to people using Instagram. New generations bring new ideas and new technology, so keeping up with the times is important. Look at me, I have an app. Ten years ago, I didn't know what an app was. Life changes, so change with it.

Building Your Team

Nobody succeeds completely on their own. Yes, I make my own real estate deals, but I have a team that helps me make major decisions and, most importantly, navigates me through areas in which I am not an expert. It's been stated many times in business that when you are looking to build your team, look for people who know what you don't know so they guide you in those areas. That's good advice.

My team members or, as I like to call them, my unofficial board, includes my general counsel. I used to have an in-house lawyer on my payroll. After some time, I decided I would be better off with a large law firm and an attorney whom I paid as needed. Matt, my attorney, has been a trusted advisor for a decade now. We talk often, and he advises whether or not to pull the trigger on many deals—he's also great at researching and finding red flags along the way. He then steers me away from potentially bad deals. My CPA along with bankers and real estate brokers are also team members, as are some successful friends in technology, one of whom helped me create Fuzul. I wanted to build an app, and they knew far more about that than I did.

The people on my team let me pick their brains, and they pick mine. These are people I trust and who understand who I am and my goals and dreams. Successful people have an inner circle that they can depend on. In my case, I also want the people in my inner circle to

Making Opportunities
Matt Paskerian, Real Estate Attorney

Manny is great at what he does; he's both smart and creative and very good at choosing markets and making opportunities where they don't exist. My favorite example is when Manny bought an expensive $29 million property in Newport Beach. The city limited the amount of rentable square footage he could have and the downstairs tenant, a steakhouse, took up a lot of the square footage.

So, to add value to the property, Manny took over the patio. It didn't have permanent windows and was not considered rentable space by the city. So, he took a common space worth essentially zero dollars and turned it into his cigar club known as the Cubano Room. He added power windows and a door separating it from the remaining common space. By doing this, he was able to generate an additional $10,000 per month in addition to the restaurant and over 40 offices in the building, which are all filled. Those are the kinds of things he does. He can see an opportunity and turn something that was worth nothing into something valuable.

▲ chapter 10 / building your brand and building your team

know that I can be there for them as well. Remember, I like helping people. That's just who I am.

As you progress in business over the years, you will also build a team of people in different industries that you can tap into as needed. This is why it's so important to network and build relationships. I've met people through social media and through referrals by the many people with whom I've done business. I find that the most significant relationships usually come through personal introductions from friends or my closest team members. While you can meet people on sites like LinkedIn, I find the platform to be more useful for checking up on the people to whom you have already been referred. It's a great place to research and read up on someone. Of course, you'll have to establish a rapport and find out about their credibility and integrity on your own. The more well-connected you become in your field, the more likely you can talk offline with people who know those referrals.

Besides being experts in their fields, you want team members who not only have your back, but can also give you honest feedback. You also need people who are accessible and are a good match for your personality. For example, if you know a very pessimistic person who always thinks the world is coming to an end, and you are an upbeat optimistic person with a positive outlook on life, you're probably not going to be helpful to each other. No, you don't need a cheerleader, but you do need someone who can match your temperament and enthusiasm, someone you can have synergy with.

Your team should know your goal and vision well and be able to help you build or enhance your brand as needed. If you don't have time to market your brand to the world, add a marketing expert to your team. There are many excellent social media marketers out there today. However, with such a glut of online marketing, it's to your benefit to also market yourself and your business directly to the people. Find ways to meet people and interact—attend conferences and industry events.

Building a brand and marketing that brand is a way of presenting your personal identity and/or business identity to the world-at-large hopefully to the prospective buyers of whatever you are selling. This could be selling dreams like Ferrari or a slew of products like Amazon.

Your team members are then along for the ride as your co-pilots. You need to let them help you navigate as you move forward to reaching your goals, your dreams, and your destination.

 YOUR ROADMAP TO SUCCESS

▶ Build your personal brand based on who you are and what makes you unique.

▶ Build your business brand based on what you are selling, what you believe in, who your customers are, and what differentiates your business from others.

▶ Make sure you are trustworthy, honest, and can maintain a credible image.

▶ Use social media, promotional items, and a variety of means to market your brand.

▶ Don't stop marketing once you've had some success. Keep marketing and change with the times.

▶ Build a team around you who can advise you on various areas of business, especially in areas that are not your strength.

▶ While you will be hiring some people to be on your team, make sure you have people who will be honest with you.

11

giving
back

always had a strong sense of the importance of helping other people. Unfortunately, when I was younger I didn't have the time or the money to do very much. As I became more aware of the needs of so many people, I got involved with several organizations, one of which was Water.org. The organization provides safe water to developing countries that don't have access to clean water or sanitation. It's an organization with a great mission. I remember doing a fundraiser for them at a resort and wanted to do something fun, so I brought over part of my car collection along with some exotic cars owned by friends of mine and displayed them on the lawn at the resort. We also had live music, catering, and a live auction for high-end jewelry by Graff Diamonds. It was a huge success, as we raised $165,000.

As I mentioned earlier, I also became very involved with TACA (Talking About Curing Autism). I have been involved with them for over ten years and feel both the gratification of helping children and the frustration that we can't do more. Leyla has joined me helping with TACA activities, and we are both active with the Children's Hospital of Orange County (CHOC). We try to do a lot of fundraising activities for these wonderful organizations. In January 2015, Leyla co-chaired the annual gala for CHOC at the Island Hotel in Newport Beach that included a gourmet dinner and John Legend as a special guest. We've both been involved in many fundraising events for both TACA and CHOC, and it's always heartwarming to inspire other people to give their time and money. In the end, it feels so worthwhile when you see that you've raised a lot of money to help children in need.

I also consider part of my time on social media as charity—I have a lot of young people who follow me, and I try to interact with them as often as I can. People ask me questions, and I try to be helpful and motivate them. I cannot necessarily solve their problems, but I can provide motivation and suggestions to keep them on the right path.

All in all, giving provides a sense of purpose, especially when you really get involved with helping others, and especially if you can change somebody's life, even a little bit.

Working with charities has given me a different kind of happiness that I had not experienced before. When I came to this country, I didn't speak a word of English. I just tried to find my way by guessing. This is part of the reason I want to help children, and why mentoring is on my bucket list. I was fortunate to grow up in the United States and have so many opportunities. Despite enduring poverty and the insults that come from bigotry, I remained optimistic and determined to reach by dreams and goals. I saw a destination in my future and did everything I could to maintain my drive and make my dreams of success a reality and, in fact, I exceeded my dreams. Many kids are not as fortunate to be able to seize the opportunities that come their way. They deserve a chance.

At the end of the day, there are a lot of kids out there who need your help. Nothing is more fulfilling than giving! Even though I now give continuously to multiple charities each year, I feel guilty and think I should do more. After all, no matter how successful you become and

Putting Activism into Action
Lisa Ackerman, Philanthropist

TACA began in my living room in 2000 with ten families talking about curing autism. Now, we are a national organization and serve more than 55,000 families.

One of the people who joined us in 2007 was Manny Khoshbin, before he had ever met Leyla. Manny was immediately taken in by what we were doing to help children with autism. By the end of his first evening with us, he wanted to know what he could do to help.

Over the years, Manny has worked at our annual gala, which brings us about 45 percent of our revenue, plus he mentions TACA whenever he has the opportunity. He brings in auction items for us, writes checks, and even held a miniature poker event—our Hold out for Hope fundraiser—at his home during Autism Action month in 2010.

Not long after Manny joined us, Leyla came into Manny's life, and she also came into TACA. Together they have supported and donated their time at TACA events, especially Ante up for Autism. Together they have co-chaired events and shared efforts on social media to help raise awareness and much needed funds.

Manny has become a TACA Ambassador, providing education on autism and helping further TACA's mission. He always has the attitude that he wants to do more, which is so wonderful. And despite his success in the real estate world, Manny always listens and makes you feel like you are the most important person in the room.

As the numbers of children with autism continue to rise from a diagnosis of one of every 2,500 children in 1998 to a more recent survey showing one in every 36 children, we need the fundraising efforts of people like Manny and Leyla to help us raise the funding necessary to research and find new ways to benefit the many families of children with autism. Manny and Leyla are not only very giving, but they inspire other people to be giving as well. They lead by example, and I am so grateful they joined our worthy cause.

how much you have, you can't take your money and possessions with you when you pass. However, you can do a lot during your lifetime to improve the lives of others by helping them meet their needs.

Keep in mind that giving back does not have to involve money; you can volunteer at a hospital or a shelter and help by giving your time. You could also mentor someone and share your skills and advice. Anything you can do to better the life of someone else is so worthwhile. There are many ways you can give, without writing a check. The key is simply getting into a habit of giving. It is the food for your soul and inner happiness.

When looking for a cause to support, most people seek something that has impacted their family or friends. I chose to work with causes that simply touched me. I had no children when I started working with TACA, but I had an affinity for children and wanted to help them in some way. There are so many people today who are less fortunate and need our assistance.

 YOUR ROADMAP TO SUCCESS

▶ Helping others is good for the soul—it's a marvelous feeling.

▶ Consider what causes touch you, or matter most to you, and step up to help in some manner.

▶ Remember, you do not only have to donate money, you can also give your time—it's very valuable to people in need.

final thoughts for the journey

I hope you have enjoyed the journey and now feel both inspired and enlightened. Hopefully, you can use my story, and what I have learned over the years, to provide some guidance to help you achieve your dreams. It's important to remember that on your journey, you can navigate around obstacles and overcome them— just never give up. Dream big, stay ambitious, and remember that anything you really want deserves your 100 percent effort. Keep in mind that if you're giving it all you've got, then it's no longer a question of IF but rather WHEN.

If I leave you with one big takeaway for your journey as you drive forward, let it be this: the drive is challenging, fun, and thrilling. Be sure to share the road and, most importantly, help others navigate their journeys, too. Got it? Good. Now, let's ride.

bonus read: a look at manny's playbook

Before I started thinking about life in terms of a road map, I thought about it like a playbook. I still do. Who's to say you can't have both road maps and playbooks in your life!

In my first book, I laid out 12 plays for finding success in the commercial real estate world. And what I've found over time is that many of these plays apply to many kinds of businesses, and life as well. The original playbook contains 12 plays divided into three sections: Power Up, Make Your Money on the Buy, and Stay in the Game. Below, I share some of the plays that can impact your life, no matter what your business is.

Play #1: Set Your Goals

Set specific long- and short-term financial goals, making sure that your short-term goals will lead you to your long-term ones. Assess your current financial situation—as well as your risk tolerance—as both are key factors in how aggressive your goals should be.

Play #2: Get Smart, Get Credible

Knowledge is power, so power up! Analyze the economy and markets related to your business so you can invest wisely at the right time and stay ahead of the curve. For me, that meant training to become a real estate agent so I could take my game to the next level and time the markets more accurately. Last but not least, get credible. Establishing your personal and financial credibility will pave the way for every business deal you make.

Play #3: Use Your Resources

Maximize the resources available to you. Build your team of bankers, experts, and other industry professionals who will help you on the path to building a successful business. Know your financing options and find out what type of financing you qualify for so you can get the capital to keep building your dream.

Play #4: Select Your Business Type

Learn the pros and cons of all of the business types that are available in your industry. What's your style—sticking small or going big? Whether you choose a solopreneur startup, a small business with a staff, or a multi-location franchise, your business type needs to fit where you are now and be scalable for the future.

Play #5: Pick a Winner

Once you know your business type, you can narrow down the specifics of what kind of business will best fit your goals, whether they be small and local or large and multi-national.

Play #6: Negotiate from Strength

Once you get started running your business, you'll find that you need to hone your negotiation skills. Why? Because everything is a negotiation! Use your credibility to your fullest advantage. "Give to get" in your negotiations, and get the deal done. Successfully navigate every stage of the negotiation process from the first contact with a client or vendor to initial offer and then on to final agreement.

Play #7: Add Value to Your Business

Understand the value of potential in your business. Once you have established yourself with credibility and your business is profitable, raise the value of it by making improvements to processes and products and offering enhancements to your customers. For me, that meant raising the value of my properties by making cosmetic improvements, leasing up, and trimming operating expenses.

Play #8: Expand Your Horizons

Stay on top of the game by staying ahead of the curve. Identify the right time to branch out into new territories. After all, in the U.S., you have 50 unique economies and thanks to the internet, all of the information you need to grow your business is right at your fingertips! See which markets are good candidates for your expansion.

▲ ▲ ▲

This is just a quick sampling of some of the plays that have worked for me. As you can see, they make good common sense, no matter what kind of business you own. For more on these plays and how I made them work for me in the world of commercial real estate, check out the full list in *The Contrarian Playbook: How to Build Your $100 Million Real Estate Portfolio from the Ground Up* (GeniusWork Publishing, 2011).

▲ appendix / bonus read: a look at manny's playbook

about
the author

Manny Khoshbin is President and CEO of The Khoshbin Company, a privately held commercial real estate company in Irvine, California. He is personally involved in all acquisitions, dispositions, other material transactions, and maintains a hands-on management of the company, which has a commercial real estate holdings in six states.

Although his main trade of business is real estate and he sees that as his backbone, he has ventured off into other business trades. As an entrepreneur, he loves to challenge himself and maintains a dream of having a vast enterprise expanding across many businesses.

Manny resides in Newport Coast with his wife, model and beauty entrepreneur Leyla Milani, and their children, Priscilla and Enzo. This is his second book.

index

Plan Your Journey

_____

_____

_____

_____

_____

_____

_____

_____

_____

_____

_____

_____

_____

_____

_____

_____

_____

_____

_____

_____

Plan Your Journey

_____

_____

_____

_____

_____

_____

_____

_____

_____

_____

_____

_____

_____

_____

_____

▲ plan your journey

Plan Your Journey

_____

_____

_____

_____

_____

_____

_____

_____

_____

_____

_____

_____

_____

_____

_____

_____

_____

Plan Your Journey

_____

_____

_____

_____

_____

_____

_____

_____

_____

_____

_____

_____

_____

_____

_____

_____

_____

_____

Plan Your Journey

_____

_____

_____

_____

_____

_____

_____

_____

_____

_____

_____

_____

_____

_____

_____

_____

_____